Family in America

Family in America

Advisory Editors: David J. Rothman

Professor of History,
Columbia University

Sheila M. Rothman

CHILDREN & QUAKERISM

A Study of the Place of Children in
the Theory and Practice of the Society
of Friends, Commonly Called Quakers

By
WALTER JOSEPH HOMAN, Ph.D.

*A*RNO *P*RESS & *T*HE *N*EW *Y*ORK *T*IMES
New York 1972

0355472

Reprint Edition 1972 by Arno Press Inc.

Reprinted from a copy in
The University of Illinois Library

LC# 70-169387
ISBN 0-405-03864-X

Family in America
ISBN for complete set: 0-405-03840-2
See last pages of this volume for titles.

Manufactured in the United States of America

CHILDREN AND QUAKERISM

CHILDREN

&

QUAKERISM

*A Study of the Place of Children in
the Theory and Practice of the Society
of Friends, Commonly Called Quakers*

By
WALTER JOSEPH HOMAN, Ph.D.

PRINTED AT THE GILLICK PRESS • BERKELEY
CALIFORNIA • AUGUST NINETEEN THIRTY-NINE

DEDICATION

TO MARJORIE CARNEY HOMAN, AND OUR
CHILDREN EARL AND ELBURT

FOREWORD

THE original form of this book was a dissertation presented to the faculty of the Graduate School of Yale University in candidacy for the degree of Doctor of Philosophy. The author wishes to express appreciation to Dr. Luther A. Weigle, Dean of the Yale Divinity School, for his inspiration and guidance in the preparation of this manuscript. Appreciation is expressed for the coöperation of the librarians of Yale University, Haverford College, and Hartford Theological Seminary.

Special thanks is expressed to the National Council on Religion in Higher Education for its part in making graduate work a possibility. The author also wishes to express deep gratitude to his wife, Marjorie Carney Homan for her faithful help and encouragement.

ACKNOWLEDGMENTS

GRATEFUL acknowledgment is made, in addition to authors in footnotes throughout the book, to the following publishers for permission to reprint from their publications.

The Macmillan Company for quotations from: George Fox's Journal, edited by Norman Penny; Hodgkin, L. V., Book of Quaker Saints; and Jones, Rufus M., Finding the Trail of Life.

The John C. Winston Company for a quotation from: Thomas, A. C., A History of Friends in America.

CONTENTS

~~~~~~~~~~~~~~~~~~~~~~~~~~~~

INTRODUCTION

ALTHOUGH many historians have dealt with the Society of Friends and have treated with considerable detail its doctrines, organization and practices, no one has made a thorough study of the place of children in the Society. This is a singular omission, considering the unique place which children have held in the Society since the beginning. The frequent mention of children in the official writings of the leaders, and the constant and specific application of doctrinal and educational theories to children, are sufficient evidence of the importance with which they were regarded. This study is an attempt to describe both the theories which underlay the Friends' deep concern for children, and the ways in which these theories were manifested in the life and practice of the Society.

The Society of Friends, commonly called Quakers, is a religious fellowship which developed in England during the religious upheaval of the seventeenth century. The movement was a protest against the formal ritualism and the priestly authority of the Church of England; and it sought to further the principle of religious freedom. The Society did not begin as a separate sect, but it was a movement whose purpose was to bring all Christians to an actual practice of the teachings of Jesus.

The Society of Friends originated in England in 1648 and soon spread throughout that country, but Friends were by no means limited to that nation. This period in English history was the time of colonization and expansion, and the Quakers sharing in the prevalent spirit of the age, settled in Ireland, Scotland, Holland and the American Colonies. In the Colonies the Friends were most numerous in Pennsylvania and New Jersey. Throughout the history of the Society, London Yearly Meeting has been looked upon as the original group of Friends and as the great example in both theory and practice. The Friends have been a missionary people and at the present time the Society is found in Great Britain, Canada, China,

1

France, Germany, Japan, the United States of America, and the possessions of these nations.

Since there has been little significant change in the theories, and even to a large degree in the practices of Friends in regard to children, this study has been able to take into account the status of children throughout the whole range of the history of the Society. The term "early Friends" is used frequently and refers to a large group of men and women who were leaders before 1737, and whose writings were used as bases for both the theories and practices of the Society. The date of 1902 is important because it was in that year that the Five Years Meeting of Friends in America was formed. This group rejected Birthright Membership and accepted Associate Membership.

The term children has been used in the early writings in an ambiguous sense. The records of the Society, particularly the epistles[1] and books concerning children frequently use the terms "youth" and "young people" when the nature of the references indicates that these apply to the ages under thirteen years. In this book the term children usually is meant to refer to the period between infancy and early adolescence, although in a few cases the age limit, as indicated in the statements made, extends to fourteen or fifteen years.

The history of the organization of the Society of Friends is the story of the life of its founder, George Fox. He was born at Fenny Drayton, often called Drayton-in-the-Clay, Leicestershire, in July, 1624. His mother, whose maiden name was Mary Lago, was of the stock of the martyrs. His father was Christopher Fox, a weaver, who was known as "Righteous Christer."[2] A summary of the character of George Fox is given by William Penn:[3]

He was a man that God endued with a clear and wonderful depth, a discerner of others' spirits, and very much master of his own. . . . In his testimony or ministry, he much laboured to open Truth to the people's

---

1. The epistles are letters or statements sent out to the various monthly, quarterly and yearly meetings by London Yearly Meeting. The first was issued in 1658 and others were sent out at irregular times until 1681. From that date epistles have been sent out each year. The epistles reported on the condition of the Society of Friends; set forth the beliefs of the Society; suggested a program of activities, particularly in regard to the relief of the Friends' prisoners and the poor in the early days of the movement; and they gave considerable advice for the education of children in religion, morals, secular subjects and manual arts.

2. Fox, George, Autobiography, pages 65-66.

3. Ibid., pages 51-55, testimony given by William Penn.

understanding, and to bottom them upon the principle and principal, Christ Jesus, the Light of the World, that by bringing them to something that was of God in themselves, they might the better know and judge Him and themselves. He had an extraordinary gift in opening the Scriptures....But above all, he excelled in prayer....The most awful, living, reverent frame I ever felt or beheld, I must say was his in prayer. Truly, it was a testimony he knew and lived nearer to the Lord than other men....He was of an innocent life, no busy-body, nor self-seeker, neither touchy nor critical. He was an incessant labourer, unwearied, undaunted in his services for God and his people.

From his earliest days, George Fox was a person of a religious nature and some of his relatives wanted him to become a priest in the Church of England. But Fox disliked the formalism and methods of the Established Church. He went to many priests and "professors,"[4] but found no help in them. He broke with the Established Church and after a long period of searching he found religious satisfaction. He came into contact with groups of Seekers, a people who like himself, had broken with the Established Church, and who sought God in solitude.

These Seekers had little or no organization. They met in silence and followed the leadings of God. George Fox had the strength of conviction and the ability of organization to win them to his cause and to become their leader. Many of these and other independent groups joined Fox. Within a few years, sixty of the Seeker preachers had become associated with Fox. They came to be known as the First[5] Publishers of Truth.[6] Thousands of people were "convinced" through their ministry, and the Society of Friends was formed.

This fellowship of Christians has been called by various names. At first they were called Children of Light. Later they came to be known as The Friends of Truth. Finally the official name came to be The Society of Friends. They often refer to themselves as the Society. The term Quaker was applied in scorn. The following explanations for the term have been given:[7]

---

4. Fox uses the term "professors" to mean those church members, whom he believed, "did not possess what they professed."
5. For the names and works of this group of preachers, see Norman Penney, "The First Publishers of Truth."
6. The term "Truth" was used by the early Friends to denote the belief or doctrine of the Society. It also came to mean the cause or purpose which stimulated the work of the Friends. In the propagation of the Truth, Friends often suffered imprisonment and harsh treatment.
7. Sewell, William, History of the People Called Quakers, Volume I, page 42.

Gervas Bennet, one of the justices of the peace and an Independent, hearing that George Fox bade him and those about him to tremble at the word of the Lord, took hold of this weighty saying and with such an airy mind, that from thence he took occasion to call him, and his friends, scornfully "Quakers." For distinction sake from other religious societies, they have been called everywhere by that English name.

The story of this incident as written by George Fox is as follows:[8]

This was Justice Bennet, of Derby, who was the first that called us Quakers, because I bade them tremble at the word of the Lord. This was in the year 1650.

A somewhat different and more psychological explanation of the term Quaker is given by Robert Barclay:[9]

Sometimes the power of God will break forth into a whole meeting, and there will be such an inward travail, while each is seeking to overcome the evil in himself, that by the strong, contrary workings of these opposite powers, like the going of two contrary tides, every individual will be strongly exercised as in a day of battle, and thereby trembling and a motion of the body will be upon most, if not upon all, which, as the power of truth prevails, will from pangs and groans end with a sweet sound of thanksgiving and praise. And from this, the name of "Quakers" was first reproachfully cast upon us, which though it be none of our choosing, yet in this respect we are not ashamed of it.

The terms Quaker and Quakerism were given to the Society early in its history, and they have been used throughout the centuries. The Friends are commonly known as Quakers. The two terms are used within and without the Society with the same meaning.

It is not believed that George Fox started out to establish a new sect among the Christian denominations. When a certain Major Porter called Fox "a chief upholder of the Quakers' sect," Fox said to him:[10]

The Quakers are not a sect, but are in the power of God, which was before sects were, and witness the election before the world began, and are come to live in the life in which the prophets and apostles lived, who gave forth the Scriptures.

In this statement, Fox denied that he was interested in developing a new and separate sect. He was interested in a fellowship of people who would turn to the Light Within and live by it. He opposed the ecclesiastical system of his day with its "hireling ministry," "Steeple-

---

8. Fox, George, Autobiography, page 125.
9. Barclay, Robert, Apology, pages 335-336.
10. Fox, George, Autobiography, pages 349-350.

houses," "Tithes," and "professors." Fox sought to unite all Christians into a universal spiritual fellowship.

The definite task which Fox believed was opened to him through the leading of the Inner Light, is stated in his Journal:[11]

> I was to bring the people off from all their own ways, to Christ the new and living way; and from their churches, which men had made and gathered, to the Church in God, the general assembly written in heaven which Christ is the head of; and off from the world's teachers, made by men, to learn of Christ, who is the way, the truth and the life . . . to bring people off from all the world's religions which are vain; that they might know the pure religion, might visit the fatherless, the widows and the strangers, and keep themselves from the spots of the world.

This calling, which George Fox believed came directly from God, became the purpose and directed the practices of the Society of Friends. In the striking religious upheaval of the seventeenth century, the early Friends presented an entirely different religion than those commonly practiced. While their doctrines were not new, the social and practical nature of their religion was unusual. There was something so sincere, so dynamic about their faith that neither religious opponent nor civil authority, neither mistreatment nor imprisonment could swerve them from their convictions. They were so different that Oliver Cromwell said of them:[12]

> Now I see there is a people risen that I cannot win with gifts or honours, offices or places, but all other sects and people I can.

A recent statement from the Discipline of London Yearly Meeting[13] shows the original nature of the Society of Friends. It suggests that the early Friends did not propose a new sect, but that they looked for a "world-wide response to the message of the universal and saving Light of Christ." These early Friends came together for the worship of God, for fellowship, and for the consideration and help of their associates who were suffering.

Thousands of people throughout England, Ireland and Scotland accepted the teachings of Fox and the other early leaders, and joined in their Society. The first records show[14] that meetings were established in Leicestershire in 1644, in Warwickshire in 1645, in Not-

---

11. Fox, George, Journal, page 21.
12. Fox, Autobiography, page 215.
13. Christian Discipline, Part III, (London 1931), page VII, and the Rules of Discipline, (London 1834), page XVII.
14. Epistles, Volume I, page IV, a statement by George Fox.

tinghamshire in 1646, in Derbyshire in 1647, and in adjacent counties in 1648, 1649 and 1650, and in Yorkshire in 1651.

It was not long until other meetings were established and George Fox recommended that five monthly meetings (local congregations) be set up in London in 1667. London Yearly Meeting, which consisted of the various monthly and quarterly meetings in England, was organized in 1672. This gathering met annually for spiritual expression and growth, and for the conduct of business, particularly the affairs of the poor and the imprisoned. New England Yearly Meeting was established in 1671; Baltimore in 1672; Virginia in 1673; Philadelphia in 1681; New York in 1695; and North Carolina in 1698.

From the earliest days of the Society, the Friends suffered great persecutions. Their property and goods were seized, and heavy fines were imposed and long imprisonments inflicted. Many of the Friends died in prison. The large number of Friends in prison, and the confiscation of Friends' property made the problem of the care of the poor and especially the poor children exceedingly great. These facts, together with the large number of people who joined the Society, made more definite rules for membership imperative.

The nature of membership, for both children and adults, during the early days of the Society is a subject of controversy. There are some who believe that membership existed from the days of George Fox; others believe that it did not exist until 1737; while still others believe that an informal membership existed from the time of Fox, but a formal, stated membership did not exist until 1737. The fact seems to be that membership existed from the earliest days of the Society and that it was informal and general.

Children of Friends were regarded as members also, and they assumed responsibilities for the affairs of the Society without any formal ceremony when they were deemed, by their elders, to be sufficiently mature.

6

⊰ I ⊱

CHILDREN IN THE THOUGHT AND LIFE OF THE EARLY FRIENDS

~~~~~~~~~~~~~~~~~~~~~~~~~~~~~~~~~~~~

CHILDREN IN THE FAMILY

CHILDREN received their greatest opportunities for growth as members of the Quaker family. There, they obtained, through example and instruction, the elements of religious, moral and practical education. In the family, children grew from little individualists interested only in their own welfare and pleasure, to social members of the group. They learned to participate in the family duties and privileges. The Quaker family was known for its frugality, industry and hospitality. Children were taught these important principles of family life from their infancy. They learned to share the work and play, and the joys and sorrows of the home. These factors were important elements in their growth.

In the family group, both parents and children shared in the responsibilities. The early Friends were clear in their conception of the place of both parents and children.

Authority rested in the hands of the parents, and they were urged to keep their authority by holding their children in subjection. Friends believed that God had given this parental power, and that He would hold them responsibile for their charge. Illustrative of the position held by the early Friends, on the subject of parental authority is a statement from George Fox, who said: [1]

All children should be brought into, and kept in subjection by the power of God . . . through the breaking of the stubborn will in them, and subjecting them to the Truth; and let them all know their places, and not to give way to that which may get over you; so then you will not know how

---

1. Fox, George, Works, Volume 8, page 23.

to rule them at last. Therefore, while they are young restrain them from such things . . . keep your authority and lose not the true wisdom and understanding given you by Christ . . . but in all things keep your authority which is given you by God.

The belief that parents held divine power was commonly accepted by the early Friends. But mere authority from God was not the only relationship with Him. Friends held that God would assist them in their daily care of children. They were to call upon Him and He would instruct them in their noble task. Friends were constantly admonished to bring up their children in the fear of God, and they were to call upon Him for help.[2]

It must have been a source of consolation to these early Friends, as they brought up their children, to believe that they were under the direction of God. And it must have made a great impression upon the children when they realized that their parents sought the aid of God in their development. Such experiences must have led the children to believe that God was near and that He was interested in their welfare. No doubt the children heard their names mentioned in prayer and God became a reality to them.[3]

There was still another relationship to God. If at any time parental desire seemed to be in conflict with God's will, children were to obey God rather than their parents. This, no doubt, applied to the time when children reached the age of maturity or of personal deci-

---

2. The epistles abound in such advice. For examples see the Epistles of 1704, 1709 and 1735.

3. From modern sources, yet in the spirit of the early Friends, the following illustrations are given: Rufus M. Jones in his remarkable book, "Finding the Trail of Life" tells of a time when he had broken some rule of the family, his mother took him aside and prayed. He said: "To my surprise my mother took me by the hand and led me to my room; then she solemnly kneeled down by me, and offered a prayer which reached the very inmost soul of me. . . . It was one thing to hear prayer in the meeting house, or in the assembled family, but quite another thing to hear my own case laid before God in words which made me see just what I was, and no less clearly what I ought to be." (Pages 109-110.) On the reality of God, Dr. Jones said: "God was just as real a being to me all through my early childhood as was any one of the persons in our nearest neighbor's house. At home He was talked with every morning and spoken of all day in a variety of ways. If any sort of a crisis was near us His help was asked in as simple and confident a way as we asked a neighbor's help when we needed it." (Page 102.)
Allen Jay wrote in his Autobiography, page 25: "I do not remember much of that prayer (his father's), but the words 'God bless Allen and make him a good boy,' have followed me over land and sea. I pity the child who has never heard his father pray."

8

sion, and it did not apply to small children. God was considered as the supreme and final authority.

Quaker parents did not rule as cruel tyrants. Rather, they stood as God's agents in directing the growth of children who were God's heritage. Parents held authority, but they were to command in love and justice. They were to be governed by the spirit of God. The single word which seemed to define the parental authority and express its methods was LOVE. Through the love of God within themselves, they were to rule the family, and through His love they were to find power.

The great task of parents was to bring up their children in the love and honor of God, according to the Truth as held by the Society of Friends. This, of course, implied that children would be given a "guarded education." They would be kept from "the vain fashions of the world" in dress, language and amusements. Children were not to be given means of extravagances, but they were to be taught a life of simplicity. One of the most important tasks of the early Friends was to train their children in keeping with the beliefs of the Society in these matters.

Parents were urged not to be indulgent with their children. There was the general belief among Friends that too much liberty was not good for children. They thought that children should be brought up to respect the desires and authority of their parents. One of the early writers had much to say about "indulgent parents" when he wrote: [4]

I have, with sorrow, seen some foolishly indulgent parents, who were so blind as not to see faults in their children, or if they did see them, through excessive indulgence would not restrain them, which in the end has proved their ruin. And yet I have known some Friends, who have gone under a religious concern to such parents, to give them advice, who instead of taking it well, have been so blind and stupid as to have returned undue reflections; and others, again who have taken it better, would excuse themselves with the most plausible reasons they could invent, saying, the child is wild and playful, and they do not like to correct it as it has a weak constitution.

This passage, written in 1688, is one of the most refreshing glimpses we have of the human side of the early Friends. One can picture a solemn elder gravely calling upon some members of the meeting and telling them that he had a "concern" to give them some

---

4. Barclay, John, The Life of Joseph Pike, pages 15-16.

9

advice on how to bring up their children. The boys had, perchance, been disrespectful to him, or they may have been caught in the flagrant act of stealing apples or throwing snowballs through a window. How grieved the elder must have been when the parents seemed to resent his help or tried to palliate the offense. "It has a weak constitution" seems to have been the stock equivalent of our current excuse, "he is such a nervous child."

Another responsibility which rested upon the parents was the fact that they were to be good examples. Since the family held such an important position in the lives of children, parents and elders were required to live in accordance with the Christian ideals which they presented to their children.

The epistles frequently[5] gave advice to parents, warning them that they should be good examples to their children. They were to stand as living illustrations of the Truth as applied to life.

The parents were examples in the daily routine affairs of life. The work on the farm and in the home was illustrative of Quaker faith. The great virtues such as truth, honesty, loyalty and dependability were practiced constantly. The mother, in the home, organized the work with regularity and system. The father managed the farm with integrity and diligence. Each member of the family had his particular duties, and all worked together for the good of the group. This was an excellent example for the children, and they learned many of the great and necessary values of life from the good practices of their parents.

It is reasonable to believe that the conversations of the family were exemplary and beneficial to the children. In the early days of the Society many Friends suffered beatings, the loss of property and long imprisonments for the sake of their religious faith. Perhaps the Friend on the next farm had been imprisoned, his goods taken and his family left in great need. This became the subject of conversation and the stimulus for active service. The children listened intently and learned to admire the strength of character of their neighbors. They desired to help in the giving of aid and they shared this joy with their parents.

The responsibilities of parents are well-summarized by Edward Burrough, when he said:[6]

5. For example see Epistles of 1709 and 1735.
6. Burrough, Edward, The Memorable Works of, page 221.

And all ye masters and heads of families be examples of all good in your families unto your children and servants; rule in authority in the fear of God, but not in tyranny, nor a rigorous mind: teach and instruct in fear, and not in cruelty; give no bad example in pride, vain-glory, drunkedness, whoredom, dissimulation, nor any other thing, but stand as a terror over evil, and as encouragers of all good; bind not the conscience of any under your way; be pitiful towards your children and servants, and pass by offenses rather than punish them with cruelty; . . . let no want be in your families, but that which is honest and right.

Children, also, had their responsibilities in the family. Their chief duty was to obey their parents. They were to recognize parental authority. There was little opportunity for the children to act according to their own desires. Nor was there opportunity for counsel between parents and children. Children were not to ask why, nor suggest plans. Their task was to follow the will of their parents. There would come a time, however, when parental authority and responsibility would cease, and the main obligation would be upon the children themselves. The parents had the problem of showing the children the right way, and were to be good examples to them, but finally the matter of choice rested upon the children. The parents would be held responsible for the right direction of children, but the children themselves were responsible for living according to the Truth.

Robert Barclay, in establishing the basic principle which directed the parent-children relationship, took his authority from Scripture. This relationship was treated in his Catechism in the form of question and answer. In this regard, he gave the following principles: [7]

Question: What good admonitions give the Scriptures as to the relation betwixt parents and children?
Answer: Children, obey your parents in the Lord, for this is right. Honour thy father and mother (which is the first commandment with promise) that it may be well with thee, and thou mayest live long on the earth. And ye fathers, provoke not your children to wrath; but bring them up in the nurture and admonition of the Lord. (Ephesians 6:1-4.) Children, obey your parents in all things; for this is well-pleasing unto the Lord. Fathers, provoke not your children to anger, lest they be discouraged. (Colossians 3:20-21.)

Barclay developed three principles underlying the parent-child relationship. These were: authority rested with the parents; both parents and children had responsibilities one to the other; and chil-

---

7. Barclay, Robert, A Catechism and Confession of Faith, page 58.

dren were to obey their parents. The relationship was a coöperative enterprise, and both parties were to give and receive.

The early Friends' ideas in regard to the care of children may be reduced to a set of rules for the discipline of children. First, it should be considered from the standpoint of the parents, and secondly, from the standpoint of the children.

The responsibilities of parents were as follows:

1. The parents held authority.
2. Parents were to be worthy examples in wisdom, moderation, and plainness in language and habits.
3. Children should be brought into and held in subjection.
4. Children should be trained in the fear and wisdom of God.
5. Parents should deal with their children in kindness, justice and love.
6. The individuality and nature of each child should be considered.
7. Parents should not rule in tyranny or cruelty.
8. Parents should guide against sin.
9. Parents should encourage the good.
10. Parents should not be indulgent with their children.
11. God would help parents in the task of training their children, and parents should turn to Him for guidance.

The responsibilities of children were as follows:

1. Children should honour and obey their parents.
2. Obedience of God superseded obedience of parents.
3. Final responsibility for right living rested upon the children and not upon the parents.

Family Worship

FAMILY worship held a regular and helpful place among the early Friends. All the family, including parents, elders, children and servants, were expected to attend and enter into the spirit of the occasion.

The worship consisted, primarily, of periods of silent waiting before God. At times the Scriptures were read and vocal prayers were offered. The service was not "planned," nor did it follow an outline furnished by some outside authority, but the family waited in silence for the "leading of the Spirit." Before each meal the family waited in silent thanksgiving to God. This, among the Friends, took the place of a formal, recited grace.

The best way to appreciate the atmosphere of such worship is to get the picture presented by Rufus M. Jones in the story of his early life. The time of which he writes is, of course, much later, but the form and spirit of Quaker worship have remained the same throughout the years. The experience of Rufus Jones was a rather typical experience of children in the Society of Friends, and could have taken place in the early days of the Society.

In regard to his own personal experience in family worship Rufus Jones says: [8]

I was not "christened" in a church, but I was sprinkled from morning till night with the dew of religion. We never ate a meal which did not begin with a hush of thanksgiving; we never began a day without a family gathering, at which mother read a chapter of the Bible, after which there would follow a weighty silence. These silences, during which all the children of our family were hushed with a kind of awe, were very important features of my spiritual development. There was work inside and outside the house waiting to be done, and yet we sat there hushed and quiet, doing nothing. I very quickly discovered that something real was taking place. We were feeling our way down to that place from which living words come and very often did come. Some one would bow and talk with God so simply and quietly that He never seemed far away. The words helped to explain the silence. We were now finding what we had been searching for. When I first began to think of God I did not think of him as very far off. At meeting some of the Friends who prayed shouted loud and strong when they called upon Him, but at home He always heard easily and he seemed to be there with us in the living silence.

In family worship perhaps greatest opportunity was given for the personal, religious development of children. This was their first introduction to the subject and experience of religion. Here they found, from first-hand knowledge, the meaning and application of religion and particularly of worship. It was a part of the order of the family quite as much as other regularities were.

Parents and those in charge of families were advised by the epistles to watch carefully that family worship was observed. Special warning was given that children should attend such worship periods.[9] The Yearly Meeting advised that the worship should be upon the basis of silence and "waiting upon the Lord," and freedom for par-

---

8. Jones, Rufus, Finding the Trail of Life, pages 21-22.
9. For examples see the Epistles of 1706, 1709, 1731, 1734, 1735.

ticipation was to be given to all. Parents were advised to read the Scriptures often within the family circle, and they were expected to tell the children of the history and beliefs of the Society of Friends. The children were to hear of the great leaders of the Society, and thus come to a knowledge and appreciation of the group to which they belonged.

George Fox believed that one of the greatest opportunities for growth in religion was in family worship. He frequently reminded parents that the task of conducting family worship was one of their great responsibilities. As he went about his task of preaching, he often held meetings of worship in family groups, and he advised other ministers to do the same thing.

What a deep and lasting impression it must have made upon children when they heard George Fox and other early Friends, within the family circle, tell of their religious experiences! How their loyalty to the Society must have developed when they heard of the heroic acts of the elders of the meeting! It is no wonder that children carried on the meetings when their parents were in prison. The children had experienced wide training in the method of conducting a Friends' meeting. They had waited in silence, and had understood its method and realized its value. Thus the children became well-trained in the spirit and nature of worship.

In writing to families, in regard to worship, George Fox said:[10]

It is desired that all Friends who have children, families, and servants train them up in the pure and unspotted religion, and in the nurture and fear of God; and that frequently they read the Holy Scriptures, which is better than to be gadding abroad. And exhort and admonish them that every family apart may serve and worship the Lord as well as in public.

It is said of Christian Barclay, the wife of Robert Barclay, that:[11]

When her children were up in the morning and dressed, she sat down with them before breakfast, and in a religious manner, waited upon the Lord, which pious care, and motherly instruction of her children when young, doubtless had its desired effect upon them; for, as they grew in years they also grew in knowledge of the blessed truth, and since that time some of them are become public preachers thereof.

The responsibilities of family worship were to be shared by all members of the group. All came on an equal basis, and all were in

10. Janney, Samuel, Life of George Fox, page 495.
11. Tract Association of Friends, Tract number 98, page 6.

need of divine guidance. By precept and example, the children learned to have true worship experiences. They became familiar with the Scriptures and with the history of the Society of Friends, and of the lives of its leaders.

In the intimacy of family worship, children learned to present their needs to God and to thank Him for His kindness to them. They set before Him, as did their parents, the trials and problems which came to them. God was presented, not as a far-off ruler, but as a loving Father who was near to the children and was interested in their welfare. The children's relationship to God became real and vital through the experiences of family worship.

William Penn wrote an article entitled "The Christian Discipline of the Family," in which he gave definite suggestions for the "well-governed family." It is interesting to note the important place which he gave to worship. The day began with "waiting upon God." Life was not to be so filled with the affairs of living that time could not be taken for spiritual growth. Penn emphasized the practice of a well-planned household. Each member of the family was to have his particular duties. All were to work together for the good of the entire household. The family was to be an expression of Christian idealism.

Family Visits

A COMMON practice among the early Friends was the system of family visits. The meeting appointed "weighty Friends" to visit families and remind them of the advices and epistles issued by the meeting, or the visitors were to talk to the family in regard to any problems which they felt should be considered. A minister or layman might have a deep concern to visit families in nearby or distant communities. Such a person would present his concern to the meeting to which he belonged, and if the meeting consented, it would give him a minute (an official statement) granting him permission to make the desired visit. Sometimes two or more Friends united in such a concern and made the visit together.

The purpose of family visits was primarily religious, or at least they were motivated by a religious concern. When the "visiting Friends" came to a family, all the group would come together and, after a period of silence, all the family would wait for the Friend or Friends to express the concern upon which they had come. Usually, the concerns had to do with the spiritual welfare of the members of the family, or such a visit might be for the purpose of Christian advice in regard to moral or other questions. If the visiting Friend had a feeling that the children were not being trained according to Truth, or if they lived contrary to its teachings, that might be the subject of the visit.

The Epistle of 1708 defined the system of family visiting as follows: [12]

It is recommended that weighty and sensible Friends of unblameable conversations be chosen, in the wisdom of God, to visit the families of Friends in His love; who are desired to advise or admonish in the peaceable spirit of Truth, as occasion may be seen.

This system of family visits was valuable in proportion to the character and personality of the Friends who made the visits. At times the visitors may have been very helpful to the children, while again they might not have helped the conditions. In all events, this practice was common among the Friends, and no doubt it made a great impression upon the children.

Visiting Friends were often away from their own families for weeks or months at a time. The children of such Friends saw the worthy example of parents who were willing to sacrifice family and other duties for the sake of answering the concern to visit families.

This practice of family visiting was very similar to pastoral calling. It brought representatives of Meetings and families together in intimate relationships. The visitors shared their concerns with the family, and the family poured out their problems to the visitors. Family visits were times of mutual, spiritual growth.

There were some, however, who looked with disfavor upon the system, but they probably had some unhappy experiences as children. This was quite possible with the many different types of Friends who had "concerns" in regard to the welfare of the children. The success or failure of family visits depended upon the personalities and methods of the visitors, and the response of the family visited.[13]

In both the theory and the practice of the Society of Friends, the family held a place of first importance for the children. The family was the institution of instruction, and the place of practical applica-

12. Epistles, Volume I, page 121. See also the Epistles for 1729, page 184.
13. The various Journals in the Friends Library tell of the trips of visiting Friends, and always speak in highest terms of the system. A book which gives a fair, critical evaluation is: Dudley, Robert: In the Days of My Youth. For a negative interpretation, see: Greer, Sarah: The Story of My Life.

tion. Perhaps neither parents nor children were conscious of the fact that these two factors were present. But, when the children came to the position of serious consideration and when they were able to make proper evaluations, they would look back upon the experiences within the family and know the great influences which it had upon their lives.

The Quaker Meeting

THE QUAKER MEETING had its origin when George Fox and a group of Seekers met in silence and waited for the foremost object of their worship—God. Such a meeting was in great contrast to the highly organized, ritualistic service of the Church of England.

In the Friends Meeting there was no priest in costly robes; there were no altar boys with swinging incense; there was no vested choir, nor deep-toned organ. There was no attempt to erect a building of architectural beauty nor symbolic insignia.

The words which define the Quaker Meeting are: simplicity, silence and freedom. The meeting could be held in a private home, in a hall, in a meeting-house or out in the open air. The place of worship held little importance. In times of suffering, when their meetings were broken up and their meeting places destroyed by soldiers and others, and the worshippers were placed in prison, the meetings were continued. The simple faith of the Friends was mystical, and worship was possible in greatest simplicity.

When meeting-houses were finally built, and Friends were permitted to conduct worship according to their belief, they remained true to the ideals of the early Friends, and erected simple places of worship. The meeting-houses were usually made up of one or two rooms. The benches were of rough, unpainted timbers, and the windows of plain glass. To the front, were the "facing seats," where the ministers of the Society sat. The similarity of apparel, the sombre and plain colors, all made for a feeling of solemnity.

The Friends worshipped God "in spirit and in truth," and based the experience upon silence. The purpose of the silence was to hear the voice of God, and be conscious of the "leading of the Spirit." In such silence the worshippers cleared the mind of all personal desires and interests, and vain imaginations and speculations, and centered the attention upon God. They believed that He would speak to them and they waited for His directions.

When God spoke there was just one requirement, and that was freedom to obey His will. The Quaker went to meeting determined neither to speak nor not to speak, but he went with an open mind to God and a willingness to do His will. When God spoke, the Friend must be free to say or do that which God had directed.

This was the setting of the Friends Meeting and children were expected to attend. Parents were frequently admonished to bring their children to both mid-week and First-day meetings. The children were to follow the example of their parents, and worship in silence, and as they grew and attended meeting, they learned to appreciate and to share more fully in the religion of Friends. While the Quaker Meeting was not organized around the interests and needs of children, yet they were expected to attend from earliest years.

The epistles warned parents and guardians of children to see that children attended meeting with regularity. A good illustration of the place of children in the meeting is given in the Epistle of 1723, when Friends are advised to keep their children: [14]

...to a constant, seasonable, and orderly frequenting, as well of week-day as of First-day meetings; instructing them to have their minds stayed in the divine gift, to wait upon the Lord therein to receive a portion of His spiritual favor; that they, from the tendering virtue of the Holy Spirit may be engaged in heart and mind to walk worthy of so great grace; and in a holy zeal to honor God, submit to bear the cross, endure the shame, and become witnesses for Him amongst the sons of men.

In some respects the children's experiences in the family worship trained them for the meeting. From their earliest knowledge, they had witnessed and had been a part of the family worship. It has been practiced in the home at all times of worship. Through the imitation of their parents, the children came to realize the method and significance of silence. When they went to meeting, they found the same kind of silence, and it came to be a common and natural part of their worship experience.[15]

---

14. Epistles, Volume I, page 165.
15. In his "Finding the Trail of Life," page 89, Rufus Jones says: "Very often in these meetings, which held usually for two hours, there were long periods of silence, for we never had singing to fill the gaps. I do not think anybody ever told me what the silence was for. It does not seem necessary to explain Quaker

The early Friends believed that not only the children, but also the servants and apprentices should be brought to meeting. The advices of early Friends,[16] and the epistles issued by London Yearly Meeting,[17] frequently urged Friends to take the young to meetings for worship. This was an important element in the place of children in the Society of Friends.

The Care of the Poor

FROM THE BEGINNING of the Society, the Friends were concerned with the care of the poor and particularly with the care of poor children. As early as 1657 an advice was sent to the meetings asking them to look after the needs of the poor of their congregations. The problem became so serious that principles were formed by the Friends, and these came to be practiced throughout the Society. Certain "poor laws" were passed by the meetings in 1710, 1721, and 1737.

In one of the earliest documents of the English Friends, and one which is of uncertain date, but probably written about 1657, the following statements were made in the form of advices for the various monthly meetings of Friends: [18]

That collections be timely made for the poor, for relief of prisoners and other necessary uses as need shall require.

That care be taken for the families and goods of such as are called forth into the ministry or who are imprisoned for the Truth's sake.

As early as 1659, in the first epistles of the Society, the meetings were urged to care for the poor in their membership, and take up "collections" for the same.[18] It was urged that the children of the poor be given "honest employment" which was consistent with the beliefs of the Society. Each meeting was requested to care for its poor children also, by providing suitable education for them.

George Fox was deeply concerned with the care of the poor children. He believed that these children, as well as those of wealthier Friends, were the "heritage of the Lord" and that they should be cared

---

silence to children. They feel what it means. They do not know how to use very long periods of hush, but there is something in short, living, throbbing times of silence which finds the child's submerged life and stirs it to nobler living and holier aspiration."

16. See George Fox, Works, Volume 8, pages 22-23.
17. See Epistles of 1723, 1729, and 1736.
18. Both references in Friends Library, Volume 2, page 409.

for by the Society. He urged the meetings to make proper provision for the poor.[19]

This interest in the care of poor children led to the care of orphans and fatherless.[20] The monthly meetings had definite responsibilities in the care of such children. It was recommended to the meetings that they should have special oversight of the estates of orphans. The inheritances of such children were to be recorded by the monthly meeting to which the children belonged, and the meeting was to appoint worthy Friends to see that justice was done to the children. Those who were entrusted with the care of orphans' or fatherless children's estates were urged to be faithful to their charge.

There was another situation in which Friends were interested. That was in the event that a widow who had children was about to remarry. The meeting was to make inquiry and see that a just settlement had been made for the children.[21]

It is to be noted by these illustrations of the care of the children, that Friends were not merely interested in the "salvation of children for the next world." The Friends gave much attention to the welfare of children in the present, and in all problems of life. The place of children in the Society of Friends is shown, in a large measure, by the care of poor children.

CHILDREN IN THE FAITH OF FRIENDS

Children an Heritage of the Lord

WE HAVE thus far discovered the place that children held in the life of the early Friends both in the family and meeting, and have shown how thoroughly children were permitted to participate in that life. This was no mere accident of circumstances. This full participation

---

19. Fox, George, Works, Volume 7, page 342.
20. This idea is stressed throughout the writings of the early Friends, especially those of George Fox. See the Epistles of 1659, 1709, 1720, 1729, etc.
21. One of the best illustrations of this principle is the example of the founder of the Society, George Fox, when he desired to marry Margaret Fell. Fox saw all of their children in the same light, and before his marriage he saw the children of Margaret Fell and knew that their mother had made proper provision for them. A most interesting account of this affair is found in the Autobiography of Fox, page 469. "The children said she had answered it to them, and desired me to speak no more of it. I told them I was plain, and would have all things done plainly; for I sought not any outward advantage to myself."

of children was justified in the minds of Friends by the most fundamental and cherished beliefs. The faith of Friends was such as to give to children a distinct status and to allow them to share in the life of the Society. Friends believed that children were an heritage of the Lord, and they thought that every child had within him the Inner Light or the Christ Within.

George Fox, the founder of the Society, developed his ideas in regard to the place of children from the Scriptures. His primary belief was based upon these words of the Psalmist: [22]

Lo, children are an heritage of the Lord, and the fruit of the womb is his reward. As arrows are in the hands of a mighty man, so are children of the youth. Happy is the man that hath his quiver full of them: they shall not be ashamed, but they shall speak with the enemy in the gate.

Since children were gifts from God, it was necessary to bring them into close acquaintance with their Maker. Fox gave the point of view of Friends when he said: [23]

And therefore, train up all your children in the nurture and fear of the Lord, that both you and they may all serve God in His spirit, in your creation and generation; for children are the heritage of the Lord, and ought to be trained up in His fear, and serve and worship Him in spirit and in truth; for it is the Lord that gave the increase of them all.

The Friends held definite ideas in regard to children's relationship to God. Primary in their teaching was the belief that children came from God. It was He that gave them, and they were the result of His power. Because of this, children were to be taught about God, and they were to think of Him as the Father of all. They were to remember that He had created them, and that He continually preserved them.

With this knowledge of God came an understanding of the nature and purpose of Christ. The Friends held the Trinitarian view and thought of Jesus as the Son of God. Children were taught that God had given them the power to choose the good or the evil, and that Christ would help them to select the good if they would listen to His voice within them. Thus, children were to be brought to a knowledge of Christ and His teachings would become their standard of living.

22. Fox, George, Works, Volume 6, page 204.
   The quotation is taken from Psalms 127:3-5.
   Fox frequently uses the expression, "children are an heritage of the Lord," and the idea has been accepted by the Friends.
23. Fox, George, Works, Volume 6, page 209.

Children's duties toward God were expressed by George Fox, when he said: [24]

Remember that you are the work of the Lord, and remember your Creator who fashioned you and formed you in the womb, and hath brought you to birth, and hath brought you to fear, and serve, and worship and honor Him, that hath made thee.

Because children were the heritage of the Lord, they were to fear, serve and worship Him. Fear, in this connection, meant to honor God; supreme loyalty was to go to Him. He was described to the children as greater than self, family, state or world. God was a Father who was interested in all the welfare of mankind. Each child was to come to know God as a personal friend and helper.

Service was the second great responsibility of children to God. Practically speaking, this meant the service of humanity. Friends emphasized activities for the improvement of social conditions and of human relations. Early in their lives, children were brought into personal contact with a socialized religion. The Quakers applied [25] their theories to the important problems of life, and children learned to participate in these situations. The children were taught social obligations in the home, meeting and school.

A third element in the children's relationship to God was that of worship. Children were taught to worship through association and imitation in the home, school and meeting. Through the long periods of silence, and by listening to the testimonies and sermons of the elders, children felt a longing within their souls. After a time they learned to know God through the experience of worship.

As children honored, served and worshipped God, they came to feel their close relationship to Him and He became a reality in their lives. This was one of the essential elements in Quaker faith for children.

Because children were gifts from God, they *shared fully* in the thought and life of the early Friends. They entered into the Society according to their own capacities of interest, judgment, reason and experience. They were placed by heredity and environment in situa-

---

24. Fox, George, Works, Volume 6, page 209.
25. Consider Friends' great contribution in the struggle for religious liberty, their three-hundred year peace testimony, their work against slavery in the United States, their child-feeding work during and since the World War. The exception to these activities, however, is the period of quietism during the eighteenth century.

tions which developed religion as taught by Friends. Children *belonged* to the Society as fully as did their parents. They were limited only by their physical, mental, social and religious immaturity. As they developed these four characteristics they shared more fully in the theory and practice of the Society of Friends.

Quakerism raised no barriers of rite or ceremony. The members relied upon the guidance and direction of the indwelling Christ, and the children learned to share in this first principle. Quakerism, above everything else, was a religion of personal experience.

Many of the principles and activities of the first century of Quakerism were not child-centered. Children were seldom objects of special consideration. Rather, they were supposed to enter as fully as possible into the religion of their elders. As one studies early Quakerism, he is led to believe that children were expected to follow adult patterns, and participate in adult religious expressions. There was *one religion* and it was shared by all, both young and old.

In the early history of the Society of Friends, there was no thought of a graded program of religious education. The children met with their parents in the long, often entirely silent meetings. There was no music or other activity to bring relief. All, including the children, were to wait patiently and humbly for the voice of God. The physiological and psychological characteristics of children were not given particular consideration. They were expected to share fully in Quakerism as it was. This was the place assigned to children who were the heritage of the Lord.

The Doctrine of the Inner Light

THE CENTRAL doctrine of the religion of the Friends was that of the Inner Light, or the Christ Within, and this affected directly their psychology of childhood. It was the belief that God is within each individual, young or old.

In answer to the question, what is the Inner Light, Isaac Penington, one of the best educated and most influential members among the early Friends, said: [26]

It is that which shineth from God in the heart, wherein God is near to men, and wherein and whereby men may seek after God and find Him.

This principle is most commonly called the Inner Light. It is,

---

26. Penington, Isaac, Works, Volume 3, page 263.

however, referred to by many different names, all of which seem to imply the same meaning. Among other terms used are the following: the Light Within, the Light, the Light of Christ Within, Christ Within, the Indwelling Christ, God Within, the Power of God in the Soul, the Voice of God, the Voice of Christ, the Seed, the Seed of God, the Seed of the Kingdom, the Spirit Within, the Spirit given to Every Man, the Spirit, the Life, the Grace of Christ, and the Kingdom of Heaven Within.[27]

All the Friends' theories, testimonies and practices originated in revelations which came through the Inner Light. The early Friends found religious satisfaction through the guidance of the Light. It directed their worship and their ministry, and it led them into communion with God, and out to the service of humanity.

George Fox himself was the outstanding example of a life based on this belief. His own spiritual growth and development resulted from the work of the Light Within. It was by means of the Light that the Truth was opened to him and he was sent forth into the active ministry. Even as a child, Fox showed a deep interest in religion. As a youth he became dissatisfied with the Established Church and sought a more personal, vital religious experience than he had been able to have in his original associations. After a long search, following conversations with many priests and "professors" of religion, none of whom gave him any help, he sought God in solitude. Fox, at the command of God, left his family and waited in silence for God. He continued in this state for about three years. During this time he relied upon the direct guidance of God, and the study of the Scriptures. He believed that he received openings from God and these directed his religious thought and practice. Fox believed that God told him that "all believers were born of God" and that each received a divine call to service in the kingdom. One of the most astonishing and often misused of his openings was: [28]

---

27. William Penn lists the following names: Light of Christ Within, Light Within, the Manifestation, the Witness of God, Wisdom, Word in the Heart, Grace that appears to all Men, and Truth in the Inward Parts. See his Select Works, page 787.
Robert Barclay gives the following: the Light that makes all things Manifest (Ephesians 5:13), the Seed of the Kingdom (Matthew 13:18-19), the Word of God (Romans 10:17), a Talent (Matthew 25:15), a Little Leaven (Matthew 13:33), the Manifestation of the Spirit (I Corinthians 12:17), and the Gospel preached in every creature (Colossians 1:33). See the Apology, page 131.
The various terms are used throughout the writings of the Friends.

The Lord opened to me that being bred at Oxford or Cambridge was not enough to fit and qualify men to be ministers of Christ. And I wondered at it because it was the common belief of people. But I saw it clearly as the Lord opened it to me and was satisfied.

Even with these revelations, he was uncertain and in distress and frequently he was tempted to turn away from his seeking. However, he continued to follow the openings as they came, and often was moved to do certain work or to go certain places. As he relied more and more upon the guidance of the Inner Light, he felt a growing confidence and after a time relief came. Of this great experience he says: [29]

And when all my hopes in them (priests and Separate preachers) and in all men were gone, so that I had nothing outwardly to help me, nor could I tell what to do; then, oh then, I heard a voice which said: there is one even Jesus Christ that can speak to thy condition.

The crisis had passed. George Fox was a new man. From that time on he followed the directions of the Inner Light.

Now that Fox had found a personal religious satisfaction he desired to bring others to that same realization. He believed that the Lord gave him his task. He thought that he had been called of God to bring people to a knowledge and use of the Light. He was to turn them away from the "vain worship" as practiced generally, and lead them to a silent waiting upon God.[30] He emphasized the fact that the Inner Light would "lead to all Truth" and that men might find salvation through following its guidance.

As George Fox continued to follow the Light and went forth in his ministry, he found others who had turned to the Light Within. They joined ranks with him and accepted as their basic principle, the doctrine of the Inner Light.[31]

---

28. Fox, George, Journal, page 6.
29. Ibid., page 8.
30. For his own story of the divine call, see his Autobiography, pages 102 to 109. He began: "I was sent to turn people from darkness to the Light, that they might receive Christ Jesus."
31. The fact that the Inner Light was the central principle of the Society was held by all writers among the early Friends. William Penn calls the Inner Light, "the main distinguishing point or Principle." (Brief Account of the Quakers, page 21); William Sewell calls it "the chief Principle." (History, Volume I, page 315); Robert Barclay, in the Apology devotes two entire sections to it. (Apology, pages 109-188); George Whitehead spoke of the Inner Light as "the means of repentance and redemption." (Tuke: Memoirs of George White-head, Volume II, Appendix, page 190); James Naylor spoke of it as "the Light of Salvation." (Sundry Books, page LV.) Throughout the four volumes of

A part of the function of the Inner Light, thought the early Friends, was to give complete knowledge of self and to lead to the highest possible, personal development. Through the guidance of the Inner Light, the individual could know his present condition, and find his future possibilities.

The Inner Light did five things for the individual who followed its leading: it led to a knowledge and appreciation of God; it brought the individual to a sight of and conviction of sin; it caused the person to have a deep repentance and a desire to do better; it took him to a state of redemption; and it directed the individual to the best possible life.[32]

The Inner Light was very practical in its direction and dealt with the common problems of life. The Friends believed that the Light, if followed, would lead people away from such evils as: stealing, drunkedness, adultery, lustfulness, vanity, injustice, oppression of others and the life-problems faced in daily living.[33] It was believed that the Inner Light would lead away from the evil to the good and noble things of life.

Robert Barclay went so far as to say: [34]

He in whom Christ the Spirit of God dwelleth, it is not in him a lazy, dumb, useless thing; but it moveth, actuateth, governeth, instructeth and teacheth him all things whatsoever are needful for him to know.

During the last quarter of the seventeenth century, there arose among Friends a conflict in which the subject of the Inner Light held an important place. The controversy centered around the idea that the Christ Within was not sufficient means of salvation. In addition to the Christ Within, there was need for a belief in the physical, historic Christ.

---

his Works, Isaac Penington writes of the Inner Light and shows his own dependence upon it, as well as its use, generally, in the Society of Friends. George Fox based his entire philosophy of religion upon it. The Epistles abound in references to it, especially to children as shown in the Epistles of 1717, 1727, 1735, and 1737. The Inner Light has remained the central principle of the Faith of the Friends. See such modern writers as William Braithwaite, A. Neave Brayshaw, Rufus M. Jones and others.

32. This view is set forth by Robert Barclay in the Apology, pages 54-55. William Penn, in the Brief Account of the Quakers, page 137, and in his Works, Volume II, pages 855-856 states the same idea. It is also evidenced in the lives of all the early leaders as set forth in the journals, memoirs and other writings.

33. Fox, George, Works, Volume 4, pages 27-28 and 73-74.

34. Barclay, Robert, Apology, pages 54-55.

The chief opponent to Barclay, Penn and Penington, the great advocates of the doctrine of the Inner Light, was George Keith who for a period of twenty years held the Quaker faith and was one of the most eloquent of the early preachers. He came into disagreement with some of the early Friends and was finally disowned by them. He was inclined to discount the function of the Inner Light and to emphasize the historical Christ, who died on the cross, and saved men through His blood.

The controversy on the subject of the Inner Light, which began in this period, led to a modification of the principle and even to a division,[35] and it has influenced the thought on the subject of the Inner Light through the history of the Society, although the doctrine still remains an important theory in the social and religious philosophy of Quakerism.

George Fox suggested that as a man believed in the Inner Light, and as he continued to obey its directions, even in a small way, his knowledge of it would increase. After the individual had gained a small knowledge of the Inner Light, and had followed its directions, it would grow in usefulness. Isaac Penington confirmed the opinion of George Fox and felt that the use of the Inner Light would be appreciated and grow slowly. The great secret was to wait upon God, and follow His guidance. As one followed the directions of the Light, new visions would come and the principle would gradually become a practical reality.

The inward study of one's self, one's thought and actions was the starting place for the knowledge of the Inner Light. To follow the Inner Light, one needed to feel a sense of unity with God, and have a desire to know and follow God's will. As one felt a sense of sin, and a desire to repent and do good, he became aware of the teachings of the Light Within. As one became able to discern between good and evil, between the things of God and the things which are contrary to God, he became conscious of the values and purposes of the Light. And it was believed that this knowledge would grow with experience.

Knowledge of the Inner Light and its leading could be known by: first, faith in God—faith to follow the Light; second, by freeing oneself from sin by repentance and right living; third, by waiting

---

35. The separation led by John Wilkinson and John Story; the disownment of George Keith; and the stress put upon revivalism in the Five Years Meeting of Friends are evidences of the influence of the controversy on the Inner Light.

upon God, waiting for His word, His time and His will; fourth, by obeying the directions of the Inner Light; and fifth, by freeing oneself from disputes and man-made thoughts and desires.

Many of the early Friends had difficulty in distinguishing between the Inner Light and conscience. It became the task of Robert Barclay to make the distinction. Barclay objected to the statements made by some, that the Inner Light was merely a part of man's natural self and was the same as conscience. He refused to believe that the Inner Light was similar to or a part of man's reasoning power.

The two great capacities of man, reason and the Inner Light, may and should contribute one to the other. Reason is rational and mental, the Inner Light is spiritual and divine. Barclay believed that the "enlightened reason" was subservient to the Inner Light, but it could be of value to the spiritual just as the physical in man could help the rational.

There was, according to Barclay, a third element in man, namely conscience. He defined it as:[36]

> That knowledge which ariseth out of man's heart from what agreeth, contradicteth, or is contrary to anything believed by him, whereby he becomes conscious to himself that he transgresseth by doing that which he is persuaded he ought not to do.

That is to say, there is something within man which tells him the right from the wrong. A standard is established, and anything contrary to that principle is considered wrong. If one commits this wrong it becomes a sin to him, and he is troubled by his conscience.

It was possible, thought Barclay, to have a good or bad conscience. It all depended upon who set and applied the standards. It was directed largely by the society in which the individual lived. Conscience would be determined, in a large measure, by heredity and environment, and these could be negative or positive. Mores of society change, and that which is right in one group is considered wrong in another. All this made conscience a rather uncertain quantity.

Barclay[37] agreed with Paul, that there was need for "a good conscience."[38] It was at this point that Barclay made the distinction between the conscience and the Inner Light. He likened conscience to a lantern, and the Inner Light to a candle. The lantern of itself

---

36. Barclay, Robert, Apology, page 143.
37. For Barclay's treatment of conscience, see Apology, pages 143-144; and 251-252.
38. I Timothy 1:5; 19.

was useless until the candle was placed in it. So, conscience needs the power of the Inner Light before it can be trusted to lead to the highest ideals of life.

Conscience, thought Barclay, was the result of reason and judgment, while the Inner Light came from God. Conscience could be blinded by false reason and wrong judgment. It could be directed by wrong standards or mores. Thus, one might have a clear—but not a good conscience. One could commit sin with a clear conscience.

But the Inner Light was directed of God. God was good and therefore everything which came through the Inner Light would be good. There could not be a bad Inner Light. The Light would always lead to the good for it came from God's goodness, love and will, and not from man's judgment, reason or will, nor was it influenced by the standards of society.[39]

The doctrine of the Inner Light was, in its very nature, applicable to children. This is true because: first, the Inner Light was found in all people; second, it was a personal experience; and third, the knowledge of and the reliance upon the Inner Light was a continuous growth.

The child could not be taught how to find and follow the Inner Light. He could not by reading about it, or hearing lectures on it, learn how to follow its directions. The Inner Light was *experienced* by each individual. Each person would have to look within himself, listen for the Voice of God, wait patiently, and then obey its guidance. Then, the child could say with George Fox: "this, I knew experimentally."[40]

The doctrine of the Inner Light was consistent with the belief that religion was a continuous, purposeful growth. The child, at birth, was not endowed with a full, complete power of the Inner Light. He

---

39. Penington said of the Inner Light: "It checks and reproves the sinner, but never consented to the evil of his heart and ways. This is of God; this is from God; this is pure; this is spiritual, not of the flesh, not of the natural; for then it might be drawn some time or other to consent to some of the corrupt desires of the natural; but though the conscience be ever so much defiled, yet the Light itself cannot be defiled. Man may set up that in his conscience which may be darkness, but God's Light can never be bribed, but will speak truly." Works, Volume 2, page 7.

40. Fox, George, Autobiography, page 82. Of his own experiences Fox said: "Then the Lord let me see why there was none upon the earth that could speak to my conditions . . . that Jesus Christ might have the pre-eminence, who enlightens, and gives grace, and faith and power. Thus when God shall work, who shall hinder? and this I knew experimentally."

was born with the Light, or at least with a capacity for the Light. As the child grew, as he learned to wait, as he felt the inner direction of God, as he practiced the guidance of the Light, as he followed the will of God, he became conscious of the power of the Inner Light. Only gradually, as he willed to follow the Light could it become of any great value.

Psychologically, the child could reach a state of "readiness" rather easily. Children live more in the realm of the mystical and the imaginative than do adults. In the play and thought life of children imagination holds a large place. For children, religion often takes the form of the mystical.[41] The relation of the doctrine of the Inner Light to children is one of the most interesting and vital elements in the place of children in the Society of Friends, and the point at which the Friends made one of their greatest contributions to the religion of childhood.

George Fox, in keeping with his theory that children are a heritage of the Lord, and in harmony with his own religious experience, believed that the Inner Light was a part of children's religious capacity. He said: [42]

Infants are enlightened with the Light of Christ . . . which believing in, they shall not be condemned, but have the Light of Life, and become children of Light. And in Christ is Light, and that is the life of men; and where there is life in an infant, there is the Light.

William Penn believed that the Inner Light had a definite place among children.[43] He believed that the Light was a part of the very nature of children. He felt a deep concern for the children of Friends that they might appreciate and practice their great religious inheritance. He pointed out that Friends' children not only had the teachings of the Society, and the good example and encouragement of

---

41. Rufus M. Jones in his "Finding the Trail of Life," pages 10-11, says: "I am convinced, too, by my own life and by wide observation of children that mystical experience is much more common than is usually supposed. Children are not so absorbed as we are with things and with problems. . . . They do not live by cut-and-dried theories. They have more room for surprise and wonder. They are more sensitive to intimations, flashes, openings. The invisible impinges on their souls and they feel its reality as something quite natural. . . . The world within is just as real as the world without until events force us to become mainly occupied with the outside one."
42. Fox, George, Works, Volume 3, page 63.
43. Penn, William, Brief Account of the People Called Quakers, pages 124-125.

parents, but far more, they had the "Principle," the Light Within which would guide them into all Truth.

Showing the universal nature of the Inner Light, one early Friend wrote: [44]

Our children and every individual in our families have the same divine Principle and sufficient Grace as ourselves, and in our obedience to it consists our common preservation.

The following is an interesting testimony in regard to the influence of the Inner Light during early life: [45]

I could say with thankfulness of heart, the Lord was my morning light; for I well remember to have been favored with that Light in very early life as a reprover for sin, even in childish transgressions and disobedience to parental injunctions. Thus it was with me when very young, that I was made renewedly sensible of the love of Him who first loved us. . . . When I committed a fault how keenly I felt reproof. I am certain that if the necessity of attending to the inward monitor were impressed upon children, they would not so often grow up in hardness of heart.

It was written of Christiana Hustler: [46]

Her attention having in childhood been turned to the Light of Christ in her own soul, she was through obedience to its manifestations, preserved from many allurements that abound in the world, and enabled to walk in the narrow way which leads to life.

It was said of Sarah Jones: [47]

When about fourteen years of age, her mind was in a remarkable degree favored with the gracious manifestations of the Light of Christ, and by following its discoveries, experienced true peace, by which she was encouraged to seek after a closer communion with the Lord. As she advanced in years, she was strengthened increasingly to give up her natural will, and to walk in the path of Christian simplicity and self-denial.

Stephen Crisp not only testified as to the nature and purpose of the Inner Light, but also showed its place in the thought and life of children, when he wrote: [48]

And surely the Lord hath an eye of tender compassion upon me, from

---

44. Kendall, John, Letters on Religious Subjects written by Divers Friends. Letter by Richard Shackleton, page 73.
45. No author given. Memorials of Deceased Members of the Society of Friends, Ann Brewster, page 82, (1843).
46. Forster, Josiah, Piety Promoted, page 34.
47. Ibid., page 31.
48. Tuke, Samuel, Memoirs of the Life of Stephen Crisp, with selections from His Works, pages 26-27.

the day that He formed me and hath appointed me to His praise; for so soon as I can remember, and so soon as I was capable of understanding, He made me to understand that which consented not to any evil, but stood in my soul as witness against all evil; and manifested that I should not lie, nor steal, nor be stubborn, nor be disobedient, but should behave myself in meekness and quietness; and set truth before me as that which was better than falsehood; and this same witness, even in the days of my childhood ministered peace and boldness unto me, when I hearkened to the counsel of it; but there was a contrary nature and seed in me that was of this world and not of God, which inclined unto evil.

The Doctrine of Original Sin

SEVENTEENTH century theology included the doctrine of original sin. It was believed that on account of the sin of Adam, all were born sinful. Those who accepted this doctrine thought that children were sinners at birth. This belief had great influence on the theories of the religion of childhood among most denominations, both in America and England.

The Friends denied the doctrine of original sin. Such belief was inconsistent with their central principle, the Inner Light. Barclay rejected original sin as an "unscriptural barbarism." [49]

The Friends believed that at birth the child was innocent. The child received his existence from God who was the "perfection of unchangeable purity," and therefore, could have "no original impurity in its nature." [50] Although the child was innocent, he was born into a world of sin. Early in his experience he would come into contact with sin, but originally he was without sin.

The child was born neither good nor bad, neither moral nor immoral. He was at birth non-moral. He was born with capacities for good or evil. Sooner or later he would have to choose between the right and the wrong.

The child was subject to heredity and environment, but he could not be held responsible for the sins of Adam, nor of his immediate parents. The Friends believed that it was impossible for a person to be guilty of sin before he had reached the age of accountability. Since the child had not attained such an age and had not been born sinful, the sins of his parents could not be charged to him. The child was incapable of breaking the law, therefore he could not be counted

---

49. Barclay, Robert, Apology, page 109.
50. Phipps, Joseph, The Original and Present State of Man, page 14.

guilty. Robert Barclay stated the Friends' position on this point, when he said: [51]

Since to infants there is no law, seeing as such they are utterly incapable of it; the law cannot reach any but such as have in some measure less or more the exercise of their undertaking, which infants have not. So from thence I argue thus:

> *Sin is imputed to none, where there is no law,*
> *But to infants there is no law:*
> *Therefore, sin is not imputed to them.*

Joseph Phipps agreed with other early Friends in the belief that the sins of the parents could not be charged to the children. On this matter he wrote: [52]

The soul of the child never was in the parent and therefore could never sin in him, nor derive guilt from his transgression. . . . To account a child guilty, or obnoxious to punishment, merely for an offence committed by its parents, before it could have any consciousness of being, is inconsistent both with justice and mercy; therefore no infant can be born with guilt upon its head.

It is clear that the early Friends believed that sin in the original nature of the child was impossible. He was not responsible for his coming into the world, nor was he guilty on account of the sins of his distant or immediate parents. The child, at birth and for a long time afterwards, was not capable of transgressing the law.

Some of the opponents of Quakerism declared that children were sinners at birth and quoted the Psalmist when he said:

Behold I was shapen in iniquity and in sin did my mother conceive me. (51:5)

Barclay refuted this attitude by saying: [53]

How they infer this consequence, for my part I see not. The iniquity and sin here appears to be far more ascribable to the parents than to the child. It is said indeed, "in sin did my mother conceive me," not my mother did conceive me a sinner.

The child became a sinner when he, himself, committed sin and not before. When he followed the evil rather than the good, when he broke the standards of religion, when he acted contrary to the law and will of God, then he was a sinner. When the child refused to follow the directions of the Inner Light, he became a sinner.

---

51. Barclay, Robert, Apology, page 106.
52. Phipps, Joseph, Ibid., pages 17-18.
53. Barclay, Robert, Apology, page 108.

The child did not have to follow the way of sin, for the Friends believed that the God who had created him had made a way of escape from sin. The Light Within would lead to a rejection of sin and the following of the good.

The Friends rejected the doctrine of original sin, and preached the doctrine of the Inner Light. They held that the Light was within every individual at birth, and that this spark of the Divine would lead the child to a personal fellowship with his Maker.

In general, the Friends accepted the belief that children were born with capacities for growth in the direction of either wickedness or goodness. It was, therefore, the task of the Friends to create an environment for children in which they would have both the desire and the opportunity to develop into a life of sinlessness, into a life of goodness. As the world was most imperfect, however, and the knowledge of sin would soon come to the child, education was necessary both to help improve the environment and to lead children to choose the good rather than the evil. The child was taught that he would "experience" a time of realizing his opportunity and his responsibility for making his own choices. If he chose the wrong, he sinned. The sin was not in his original nature but in his act of sin. Friends emphasized the belief that both individuals and society could be improved through education, and early in their history they developed a program of education in conformity with this belief.

The Rite of Infant Baptism

THE FRIENDS rejected the practice of infant baptism for three distinct reasons. In the first place, the Friends rejected infant baptism because it was contrary to their attitude towards sacraments. One objection was the fact that the term "sacrament" had been taken from the military oaths among the "heathen." Also, it had been a continuous cause of disharmony and quarreling among Catholics and Protestants. The controversy was in regard to the nature, number, value, efficacy and administration of the sacraments. Another objection of the Friends was the fact that the sacraments, as commonly practiced by the churches, had become a part of a formal ritualism. Worshippers had put their trust in the form and had lost the true meaning and value of the sacraments.

The Quakers believed that all life was sacred. They held that a full and true appreciation of the sacred would come only through the Inner Light. A sacrament, thought the early Friends, was first of all inward and spiritual. It needed no outward, physical act to make it a reality. Thus it followed that the Friends believed that baptism and the Lord's supper, or communion were not physical, outward ceremonies, but they were an inward and spiritual fellowship with God. It is not fair to the Friends to say that they did not believe in baptism or communion. They believed in and emphasized both of them. But they insisted on the inward and spiritual nature of sacraments. They relied upon the guidance of the Inner Light for a spiritual baptism and a spiritual communion. For these reasons, Friends rejected all outward symbols and rites in general, and infant baptism in particular.

In the second place, the Friends rejected infant baptism because they denied the theory of original sin. The child at birth was not guilty and therefore, did not need a baptism which would cleanse him from his sin. Even if the Friends had believed that the child was "conceived in sin," they would have objected to the practice of infant baptism because they did not believe that an outward ceremony could cleanse an inward sin.

In the third place, the Friends rejected the rite of infant baptism because it was inconsistent with their basic principle, the doctrine of the Inner Light. When the child had come to the place where he, himself, had committed sin, and therefore needed salvation, the Friends held that an outward act could not take away the sin. They emphasized the belief that salvation could come only by following the directions of the Inner Light. The Voice of God within each person would lead him to the good life and to salvation.

Since the sacrament of infant baptism is in the realm of theology, we turn to Robert Barclay for the position of Friends in regard to this rite. Barclay's analysis of infant baptism was a part of his treatment of the subject of baptism. He rejected infant baptism as a "mere human tradition" and said that it was not based upon Scripture, but was the invention of men.[54] He said that even if water baptism could be justified that would not prove the case for infant baptism, but then the problem would be to find sufficient proof for it. He also said that if baptism in general were refuted, then it naturally followed that infant baptism would have to be rejected. The Friends' view of the sacraments made it necessary to reject infant baptism.

---

54. Barclay, Robert, Apology, page 381.

George Fox believed that all sacraments were spiritual, and were realized through the guidance of the Inner Light. He said that Christ was the one who baptized the child, not with an outward ceremony, but rather within the conscience and heart.[55] He urged parents to teach this principle to their children that they might continually live by this inward baptism. He rejected infant baptism when he said:[56]

> The baptism of infants, I deny; and there is no Scripture that speaks of a sacrament but that baptism that is in Christ, with one spirit into one body. (Galatians 3:17.) That I confess according to the Scripture.

An interesting story is told of a debate between George Fox and a Roman Catholic priest. Among the topics discussed was the subject of infant baptism. The priest asked Fox if he believed in the christening of children. Fox said there was no Scripture for it, and at the amazement of the priest, Fox said:[57]

> Nay. The one baptism by the one spirit into one body, we own; but to throw a little water on a child's face and to call that baptizing and christening it, there is no Scripture for that.

Theories of Election and Reprobation, and Predestination

DURING the seventeenth century, English theology was filled with the theory of election and reprobation. There were many who believed that only a few were "elected to be saved," while many were "doomed to destruction." Such a doctrine was inconsistent with the doctrine of the Inner Light which held that every man had within him a Light which could be his means of salvation. The Friends' belief in and practice of the doctrine of the Inner Light led them to refute the theories of election and reprobation.

---

55. Fox, George, Works, Volume 8, page 172.
56. Ibid., Volume 3, page 594.
57. Sewell, William, History of the People Called Quakers, Volume II, page 156.
    For the statements of other early Friends' writers on the subject of infant baptism, see:
    Burrough, Edward, Memorable Works of a Son of Thunder, page 327.
    Naylor, James, A Collection of Sundry Books, page 46.
    Phipps, Joseph, A Dissertation on the Nature and Effect of Christian Baptism, pages 70-71.
    Tuke, Samuel, The Memorable Works of George Whitehead, Volume I, page 116.

George Fox was very definite in his opposition to these theories. He could not believe that God had wished and planned that a large portion of humanity should be doomed to final torment and destruction, while the small minority should be brought to heavenly joy and salvation. He thought that God desired that all men might be saved, and that He willed neither that some should be saved, nor that some should be lost. Fox held that God made man free to choose and that man would be held responsible for his choice. To be lost, man had to commit some sin and fail to repent. If one were to be condemned it would be on account of his own transgression. If man was saved, it would be because he had listened to the Light Within and had obeyed its directions.

In writing on the subject of election and reprobation, Fox said: [58]

Now the Lord God opened to me by His invisible power that every man was enlightened by the Divine Light of Christ, and I saw it shine through all; and that they that believed in it came out of condemnation to the Light of Life and became the children of it; but they that hated it, and did not believe in it were condemned of it, though they made a profession of Christ.

George Fox found much proof for his position in the Holy Scriptures. He used parts of both the Old and New Testaments. He found evidence in law, prophecy and philosophy of the Old Testament. He relied strongly upon the Gospels, the Acts of the Apostles, the Pauline Letters, the General Letters, and Revelation, and from these sources he made a good case against the doctrine. By the use of the Scripture Fox established three points: first, that all men have the opportunity of being saved, and that none were determined for destruction;[59] second, that the doctrine was inconsistent with the teachings and works of Jesus, Paul and the Apostles;[60] and third, that if men were lost, they reached that state through disbelief and disobedience.[61]

---

58. Fox, George, Autobiography, page 101.
59. Fox quoted: Isaiah 49:6; Ezekiel 18:21, 23, 32; Psalms 145:9; Matthew 18:11; Mark 16:16; Luke 15:7; John 1:4-9; John 3:16-17; Acts 10:34-35; Hebrews 5:9; and other passages.
60. The doctrine, thought Fox, would eliminate Jesus' Great Commission to "go into all the world"; as well as the teachings and works of Paul and the Apostles.
61. Among the passages used by Fox on the third point were: Mark 16:16; and John 3:19-21. Throughout his "Works," George Fox denied the doctrine of election and reprobation, and insisted that all men could be saved by following the guidance of the Inner Light. He, with Barclay and other early Friends, established the faith of Friends on this point, not only for the early period, but for succeeding periods of Quakerism.

Likewise, Friends rejected the theory of predestination. The subject was evidently not a serious problem since very few of the early writers dealt with it. It was so similar to the doctrine of election and reprobation that when one was rejected, the other naturally was discarded. Robert Barclay in a tract entitled, "The Serious Consideration on Absolute Predestination" gives nine objections to the doctrine.[62] These, no doubt, were accepted by the early Friends as sufficient reason for the rejection of the theory. Predestination is in direct opposition to the doctrine of the Inner Light and since the Light Within was the central principle from which all other beliefs came, it would follow that the Friends would reject any theory of predestination.

Conversion and the Second Birth

ALTHOUGH the Friends rejected the theories of original sin and predestination, and believed that the child was not a sinner until he himself committed sin; they insisted that the children needed the second birth. In most cases it was necessary for children to experience conversion.

The status of children, according to the opposing doctrines of original sin and Inner Light, may be stated as follows:

From the doctrine of Original Sin	*From the doctrine of Inner Light*
1. As children of Adam, all share in the consequences of his sin.	1. Children are born in a state of non-moral innocency and are not sinners, and they have the Inner Light.
2. Children are born into a world of sin.	2. Children are born into a world of sin.
3. Sin is a possibility for all, and all will commit it.	3. Sin is a possibility for all, but the Inner Light, if followed, will turn from sin to the good.
4. Children are naturally sinners, "conceived in sin."	4. Only through their own acts of sin do children become sinners.
5. All children must be converted. They must repent of their sins.	5. All children must experience the second birth and it is made possible by the Christ of the cross, and the Christ Within.

---

62. Barclay's objections were listed on pages 2 to 7 as follows: (1) it was not Scriptural; (2) it was not mentioned by any writers, great or small, in the

The general condition of all mankind, at birth, is set forth by Edward Burrough, when he says: [63]

Man was planted a noble vine, wholly a right seed, to bring forth good fruit unto his Maker, but he is turned into a degenerate plant bringing forth cursed fruits, which the Creator hath not pleaure in. . . . All creatures that God made, in the creation and beginning were very good in His sight that made them, and no creature was evil in its creation. But man transgressing against his Maker became evil, and did evil in the sight of the Lord.

Because they yielded to the temptations of the world into which they were born, all children needed to be converted. By conversion the early Friends meant not so much a sudden, emotional turning away from sin and evil, away from a life of shame and selfishness, away from the threat of eternal damnation but rather, they thought of conversion as an inward, spiritual growth following the guidance of the Inner Light. They were not thinking primarily of salvation from hell to heaven; they were more interested in a continuous, developing appreciation of and a reliance upon the Light of Christ Within which would lead to all Truth, and right living.

The early Friends were particularly interested in life here and now. They did, however, look forward to a happy eternity with God, but that was thought of as the result of a good life here on earth in service to their fellowmen. The statements of the early Friends in their advices, disciplines and epistles were concerned with the moral, vocational and religious education of children. Children were to be conscious of life with all of its problems. The religion of Friends was, above everything else, practical. Therefore, the function of conversion was personal and positive. Each child, with the help of parents and elders, was to make a careful examination of himself. He was to see the possibilities of evil and good which lay before him. He must have knowledge both of the world of sin, and of the power of the Inner Light. As he grew in this wisdom he gradually and thought-

---

first four hundred years after Christ; (3) Augustine refuted it; (4) Dominicus and John Calvin condemned it; (5) it is injurious to God because it makes Him the author of sin; (6) it makes God "delight in the death of sinners"; (7) it is injurious to the nature and purpose of Christ, who "through love redeemed mankind"; (8) it makes the preaching of the Gospel a mere mock and illusion; and (9) the doctrine is injurious to mankind.

It is interesting to note that John Wesley used the entire tract in his own book on the subject of predestination, and evidently accepted it as the faith of Methodists on this point.

63. Friends Library, Volume 14, page 436.

fully became converted and reached the state of the inner or second birth.

Children needed the second birth for two reasons: In the first place it would free them from their sins, clean their minds and actions, and in the second place, it would help them to know, appreciate and use the Light Within in order that they might follow the guidance of Christ and attain the highest goal of self-realization.

The Friends denied original sin, but affirmed the fact that sin exists, that the child was subject to sin, and that in the natural course of living the individual would probably commit sin. The function of conversion, therefore, was not to emancipate from some original taint or prejudice of nature for which they were not responsible, but to help them rid themselves of actual sins, to turn them to Christ and lead them into a Christ-like life.

The early Friends held that all children were born with the capacities for good or evil. They, as heirs of the first Adam, were born with capacities for sin, and as "joint heirs with Christ," were born with capacities for good. As they committed sins, they by their own acts fell from the state of good to evil. As they did that which was good, they became aware of a state of godliness.

In order that children might choose the good and forsake the evil, they needed a high, moral standard of judgment. They needed to know and to desire the good. This was possible only as they were converted and as they experienced the second birth.

The result of conversion was justification and this led to the second birth. Justification meant freedom from sin by the gift of the Holy Spirit. The justified person, said Robert Barclay, "has true and real virtue in his soul." The individual who was justified was "saved" and became a new person.

The early Friends used the terms conversion, justification and the second birth to represent the stages through which the individual passed as he came from sin to God. All mankind needed to experience these three stages to enter the Kingdom of God. In order that the individual might attain the second birth he needed to be convinced of sin; he had to desire those things which were pure, good, merciful and holy; and he would have to reach the state and thought of life which hates the evil and loves the good. He needed to look within, see the guilt and know the possibility of good. He would need to find the truth of Christ through the Light Within.

The Friends believed that the second birth was a universal need. No individual could be saved nor could he reach his highest development without regeneration or rebirth. Every child must eventually come to the place of reflection and thought which would turn his meditations inward. He must come to the place of self-evaluation, and see his life as it is.

Robert Barclay voiced this idea when he wrote: [64]

Forasmuch as all men who have come to man's estate (the man Jesus excepted) have sinned; therefore all have need of this Saviour, to remove the wrath of God from them due to their offences; in this respect He is truly said to have borne the iniquities of us all in His body on the tree.

That conversion was the necessity of children and not limited to adults was stated by William Penn.[65] He warned the children of Friends not to think that they had been converted or had attained the second birth because their parents had done so. He told them that they "must be born again" and that the Inner Light would direct them to this experience.

The Friends not only believed that the rebirth was essential for all, but it was also available to all. Redemption came through Christ, the Christ of the cross, and the Christ within. Salvation,[66] said Barclay, came only as men saw their own faults, desired to do better, repented and sought redemption through the two-fold nature of Christ.

It was believed that this second birth was possible for children as well as for adults. It was felt that the rebirth might be a struggle and many probably would try to turn the children from their quest. But if children would not turn back they would have the great experience of rebirth.[67]

The results of conversion and the second birth were certain. The person who reached such a state knew that his sins were forgiven and that he had a guide, the Inner Light, which would direct his way. All things would become new and the individual would be willing and anxious to "bring forth good fruits."

James Nayler suggested that the values of the rebirth would not be realized suddenly nor at one time, but they would continually be felt and appreciated. He urged children to continue waiting, for:[68]

---

64. Barclay, Robert, Apology, pages 194-195.
65. Penn, William, The Rise and Progress of those People Called Quakers, page 75.
66. Barclay, Robert, Apology, page 195.
67. Nayler, James, A Collection of the Works of, page 665.
68. Nayler, James, Works, page 669.

The more diligently you wait upon Him in all conditions you pass through, even so the more do receive Him by drinking in that heavenly virtue that is in Him.

As in other matters of religion, there were no separate rules or principles for children and adults on the subjects of conversion and the second birth. In this regard all were equal. All were born into a world of sin; they came to a place of sinfulness and all needed conversion. If they desired, sought and followed Christ, all could reach the state of the second birth.

Although all people were on an equal basis in these regards, conversion and the second birth were personal. Each individual must have his own experiences of them. The child must come to know his own condition; must come to a knowledge and an appreciation of the two-fold nature of Christ; and must make a personal dedication. Then he would receive the gift of the second birth.

At what age or time the child would experience the new birth was uncertain and variable. There were no established laws of averages as to the time of this transformation. The Friends did not have certain rites, tests or progressive steps which were to be completed or followed when children reached a certain physiological or psychological age. Conversion and rebirth came to the child when he was able to understand what they meant. The Quaker child's environment continually turned his attention toward these elements in religion. In home, meeting and school, children regularly came into contact with people who had been converted and had attained the second birth. These people were living according to the directions of the Inner Light. The parents and older folk of the meeting, particularly the visiting ministers, all gave evidence in their preaching and living of the nature and value of the second birth. True to their nature, children learned of the conversion experiences of others, through association. By imitation which led to a personal experience of trust in the Inner Light, the children were converted and lived in the condition of the second birth. With some children this would come early, with others it would be late, but all had opportunity to share fully in the experiences of conversion and rebirth.[69]

---

69. For additional references on the subject of conversion and the second birth, see:
Penn, William, Brief Account of the People Called Quakers, pages 1 to 5, and 27.
Penn, William, No Cross, No Crown, page 88.
Fox, George, Works, Volume 3, pages 105-106; 382; 410-421.

Some Friendly Testimonies

THERE were certain distinctive practices of Friends which were called "testimonies" of the Spirit within them, and the children shared in these habits of life. The fact that children were expected to engage in these practices shows how thoroughly the young were incorporated into the life of the Society. The early Friends believed that they were to break away from the "vain customs and manners of the world," and that they were to "walk in plainness and purity." Among these testimonies were: the simple dress, the plain language, and the method of referring to days of the week and the months of the year.

In the Yearly Meeting epistles parents were frequently instructed to train their children and families in the modesty and simplicity of dress, speech and actions. The responsibility for this training rested upon the parents. The parents were to be examples for their children and teach by actions as well as by precept. The children learned the particular testimonies through the instruction and example of their parents. The parents were reminded constantly to:[70]

train them (the children) in the nurture and admonition of the Lord in sobriety, modesty, and plainness in apparel and conversation, as becometh our holy profession and Christian religion.

The manner of dress held an important place among the testimonies. Simplicity and modesty with freedom from "outward" adornings characterized the Quaker garb. The early Friends made quite a contrast to the outward appearance of the Englishmen of their day. The clothes of the children were patterned after those worn by the adults.

The second testimony was the use of the plain language. The Friends believed that "you" should not be used in speaking to one person. Neither King nor peasant should be addressed "you." Each should receive the plain thee, thou, thy or thine. The plain language was spoken in family and meeting, in school and in store. A part

---

Ibid., Volume 5, pages 153-154; 410-421.
Ibid., Volume 8, pages 11; 179-180.
Friends Library, Volume 1, Memoir of George Fox, page 43.
Ibid., Volume 2, Life of Thomas Wilson, page 323.
Ibid., Volume 2, Life of William Dewsbury, page 272.
Ibid., Volume 5, Life of John Griffith, pages 447-450.
Ibid., Volume 14, Memoir of Edward Burrough, page 454.
Penington, Isaac, Works, pages 260-261.
70. Epistles, Volume I, page 64, Epistle of 1692.

of the child's natural environment was the use of the plain language. To have used you or yours to an individual would have seemed profane.

A third testimony was the rejection of the Roman names for the days of the week and the months of the year. The Friends spoke of the first to seventh day of the week, and the first to the twelfth month of the year. They objected to the use of the "names of the heathen gods and goddesses." The children were taught the use of numerals rather than the names of the day and month.

These testimonies were often great trials to the children. This was especially true when the children attended schools not conducted by Friends, or when they mingled in groups outside of the Society. This is illustrated by a statement made by Thomas Chalkley: [71]

> When between the ages of eight and ten years, my father sent me nearly two miles to school to Richard Scoryer. I went mostly by myself, and many and various were the exercises I went through, my beatings and stonings along the streets, being distinguished to the people by the badge of plainness which my parents put upon me, of what our profession was; divers telling me, it was no more sin to kill me than it was to kill a dog.

For many generations these testimonies were adopted and recommended by the meetings, and were taught and practiced by the family. In these testimonies the children shared fully.

71. Friends Library, Volume 6, page 3, Journal of Thomas Chalkley.

⊰ II ⊱

THE EDUCATION OF CHILDREN
BEFORE 1737

THE SYNOPTIC VIEW OF LIFE

THE WAY in which the Friends regarded the education of their children is typical of their whole point of view. They held what might be called a synoptic view of life. All life was guided by one philosophy, and there was little distinction between times and places, leisure and labor, church and state, religion and morality, education and religious education. Likewise education was not confined to schools or particular courses in the curriculum. Its object was to help the individual to see life as a whole, adjust himself to any situation, or remake the situation. In this process all the forces of home, meeting and school were combined.

The principle around which life was thus integrated was a religious one. The Friends thought that the task of each individual, as well as of society as a whole, was to know, accept and follow the will of God, as revealed by the Inner Light. The basic elements of all early Quaker education were: love of God, of self, and of society; the good life here and now; and the spirit of Christ in the thought and actions of all persons in all situations. To insure the attainment of these attitudes, parents were exhorted to attend to the religious, moral, and practical education of their children; attendance at meetings was required of children; and schools for boys and girls were established in practically every community where there were enough Quakers to support one.

As is shown in the epistles and advices, no sharp lines of distinction were drawn between the various types of education. The same epistle would advise parents to bring up their children in the fear

45

of the Lord; to teach them the plain, modest and simple methods of dress, language and actions; and to train them in some useful work.

In the educational theory and practice, children were given special consideration. It was desired that they should follow the Light Within, and through personal experience develop a Christianity according to the faith of Friends. Children were taught Friendly ideals of morality. They were given the rudiments of learning. Education did not end in some abstract philosophy, but it led to activity.

THE AIMS OF EDUCATION

AMONG the early Friends, education was considered as an integrating process. It was a continuous growth. Individual capacities and needs were considered with care, especially in the manual arts.

There were two aims of education, the ultimate and the immediate, which directed the educational processes in the family, meeting and school. The ultimate or principal aim of all education was: to instruct and train boys and girls so that they might live in the world, and be prepared for a future state, according to the religious faith of the Friends. Education was primarily life centered. The Quaker boys and girls were to learn how to live here and now. This was not a simple situation, for the early Friends were pioneers in the struggle for religious liberty and freedom of conscience. In this effort the children shared fully in the trials and sufferings of their parents. To wear the Friends' garb, to speak the plain language, and to refrain from the recreation and amusements followed by other children who were not members of the Society, were most difficult tasks. Such a life called for a serious and constant instruction. George Fox and the early Friends believed that they were to call people away from the "vanity and looseness" of that day, which led them from the respect and obedience of God. The primary task was prompted by the religious motive to lead the children to God.

In addition to this general or ultimate aim, there was an immediate aim. This may be stated as follows: to give instruction in and opportunities for personal experience and growth in religion, morals, secular education and manual arts.

Here, again, the great motivating force for education was the Friends' idea of religion. The Inner Light revealed God and His will for men. This included the children's relationships to God and to their fellowmen. It helped develop a moral standard and it directed the type and nature of intellectual study. It helped guide the children in their moral and vocational interests and pursuits.

George Fox believed that education was based upon religion and that the early training of children would have a great influence upon their later years. He said:[1]

Now this is the duty of all youth, let them be males or females, to remember their Creator, and let Him not go out of their memory, so that they may be fitted to stand in the evil days when they come; for when they grow up to be young men and women, then the evil days will appear in which they may be tempted to adultery, fornication, drunkenness, ungodliness, theft, murder, lying, cozening, cheating, unrighteousness, lightness, wantonness, and pleasures and other evils. . . . For Solomon saith, "train up a child in the way he should go, and when he is old he will not depart from it" (Proverbs 22:6). Here is the duty of parents, and the duty of children, which is to be practiced and followed.

The specific recommendation for education according to the Society of Friends was given in the Epistle of 1696:[2]

That they (children) may be trained up in Truth's way, and with a commendable education according to your abilities, that a peculiar people we may be in the life of righteousness.

It was the general opinion of Friends that religion should be the chief aim of all education. The Friends were not content to teach their children only reading, writing and other rudimentary knowledge. They believed that these were very essential, but they did not hold place of first importance. It was most legitimate to train children to become writers, mathematicians or tradesmen, but the primary object was to lead children to an inward communion with God and an outward activity in the creation of a Christian social order.

This religious motive in education was presented to the children as a gracious calling and a great challenge. The children were taught that they were to "outstrip and excel the world in virtue, purity, chastity, godliness, modesty, civility, righteousness and in love."[3] Friends emphasized the belief that they were to be a "peculiar"[4] people and their children were to be trained as such.

---

1. Fox, George, Works, Volume 6, pages 201-202.
2. Epistles, Volume I, page 87.
3. Ibid., page 20, Epistle of 1684.
4. Peculiar in the sense that the Friends were different in theories and practices of other people. There was probably some similarity to the Hebrew idea of

There was some danger in this philosophy that it might lead children to think too highly of their profession and of themselves. It tended to make them narrow-minded and somewhat self-centered. However, this attitude probably was overcome when children faced the realities of life and were made to suffer for their convictions.

A GUARDED EDUCATION

FRIENDS frequently used the term a guarded education. By this they implied two principles: first, an education in the beliefs, history and policies of the Society of Friends; and secondly, an education which was free from immoral influences.

The purpose of the guarded education was to protect children from evil influences, and to give them careful instruction in keeping with the faith and practice of the Friends. It was an indoctrination in the ideals of the Society.

While the motives back of a guarded education were, no doubt, worthy yet the principle itself has many weaknesses. In the first place, guarded education seems inconsisent with the basic principle of Quakerism, namely, the Inner Light. The directions of the meeting in regard to either religious or moral problems could be against the leading of the Inner Light. Such direction would at least have the tendency of limiting the guidance and counsel of the Light.

The principle of guarded education did away with the theory of self-realization. There was little opportunity for freedom of choice, or the expression of individuality. It is interesting to note that the Epistle of 1696 advised parents to train up their children "according to your abilities." This was according to the financial and other capacities of the parents. Nothing was said about the interests, capacities or needs of the children. It would seem that the principle of guarded education would tend to weaken rather than strengthen personality.

The sincerity of the early Friends cannot be questioned. They believed that the Lord opened to them a better way of life. They thought that they were called to revive primitive Christianity. Since they felt that they had this special commission, they believed that their great task was to indoctrinate the children and youth as well as adults, in the philosophy of life which they believed. From the

---

"God's Chosen People." The early Friends were a "different" people, at least, in their religious, moral and social beliefs and practices.

48

standpoint of zeal, profession, and earnestness, the principle of guarded education was a worthy philosophy. From the viewpoint of modern education, and the effect upon children, it is looked upon as a poor method.

One of the chief objections to the principle of guarded education is the fact that it was a conditioning process. It was a situation of complete indoctrination without the privilege of individual initiative and freedom. The teaching of a definite philosophy or theology is permissible, but if it eliminates freedom of choice it becomes an unworthy principle in a philosophy of education.

THE SOURCES OF EDUCATION

GROWTH in knowledge and experience, thought the early Friends, came from two sources. One was by revelation, and the other was through education. The Friends believed that through the Inner Light God revealed Himself to both the young and the old as they waited for guidance from Him. The early Friends went so far as to say that the spiritual values could be known only through the revelation from the Spirit of God. They held that the knowledge of Jesus Christ and the true knowledge of God, could come only through a spiritual revelation, and that this was accessible to every true Christian. All other instruction was of little value unless, first of all, one had this true knowledge of God. One needed only to wait for the guidance of the inward, spiritual teacher. On this matter Barclay said:[5]

Wait then for this in the small revelation of that pure light which first reveals things more known; and thou becomest fitted for it, thou shalt receive more and more, and by a living experience easily refute their ignorance who ask, how dost thou know that thou art actuated by the Spirit of God?

There has been a tendency among some Friends to rely entirely upon the immediate revelation of the Spirit in regard to spiritual truth. This attitude has had, in some cases, dilatory effect upon the ministry.[6] Its results have been seen in the education of children, par-

---

5. Barclay, Robert, Apology, page 72.
6. The Friends accepted the "opening" of Fox, that "to be bred at Oxford or Cambridge was not enough to fit and qualify men to be ministers of Christ." The Friends also accepted Barclay's disapproval of an educated ministry. He objected to the belief that ministers should be trained in Latin, Greek and Hebrew; in logic and philosophy and in "school divinity." He thought that

ticularly in regard to instruction in the Bible, doctrine and other teaching in religion. But in its highest interpretation this idea of the inward, spiritual teacher has had great value. Barclay and Fox and other early Friends recognized the value of education as well as of inspiration or revelation. They tried to find a proper synthesis between the two. The Friends believed that the knowledge which came through the divine revelation was the highest possible knowledge; but such information was the starting point for fuller growth. Instruction and added knowledge were not only helpful but essential.

George Fox, did not have much institutional training, but throughout his life he was a student. His sermons, discussions and writings, particularly his journal, reveal, in many ways, an unusual knowledge and insight of spiritual things, a profound use and interpretation of Scripture, and a keen interest in education in general.

Fox welcomed educated men into his fellowship. Such men as Robert Barclay, Thomas Ellwood, George Keith, Isaac Penington and William Penn were very well-trained men, and all held most important places in the Society of Friends during the seventeenth century. Their writings hold place of supreme importance in the literature of the Society. Their active ministry set the ideals of the movement throughout its entire history. Their standards of education for children, not only led to the establishment of a system of education among the Quakers, but they set forth principles which are a part of modern educational philosophy. They were educational leaders, they were educated themselves and they had deep concerns for the education of children.

William Penn, in his "Fruits of Solitude," of which he writes, "I present thee the Fruits of Solitude, a school few care to learn in, though none instructs us better," has a section on education. In this he wrote: [7]

> We are in pain to make them scholars, but not men! To talk, rather than to know.

---

the true ministry was inspired by God's spirit. For details see the Apology, Proposition X, "Concerning the Ministry."

Fox said: "I was to bring people off from . . . all their beggarly rudiments, with their schools and colleges for making ministers of Christ, who are indeed ministers of their own making but not of Christ's." (Journal, pages 21-22.)

Throughout their history, Friends have never had official, educational requirements for ministers, although their colleges and schools have Departments of Religion.

7. Penn, William, Works, pages 820-858.

The first thing obvious to children is what is sensible; but that we make no part of the rudiments. We press the memory too soon, and puzzle, and strain, and load them with words and rules; to know grammar and rhetorick and a strange tongue or two, that ten to one may never be useful to them; leaving their natural knowledge uncultivated and neglected; which would be of exceeding use and pleasure to them through the whole course of their life. To be sure, languages are not to be despised or neglected. But things are still to be preferred.

Children had rather be making tools and instruments of play; shaping, drawing, framing and building . . . than getting some rules of propriety and speech by heart. . . .

It were happy if we studied nature more and in natural things, and acted according to nature; whose rules are few, plain and most reasonable. Let us begin where she begins, go her pace, and close always where she ends, and we cannot miss being good naturalists. . . . The creation would not be longer a riddle to us: the heavens, earth and waters with their respective, various and numerous inhabitants. And it would go a great way to caution and direct people in their use of the world, that they were better studied and knowing the creation of it. . . .

It is of interest to note that William Penn's philosophy of education issued in the early days of the Society of Friends is similar, in many respects, to certain principles emphasized in modern education. One can easily interpret Penn's viewpoints by using such common educational expressions of today as: life-centered, "continuous, purposeful reconstruction of experience," "activity leading to further activity," progressive, development of personality, self-realization and "education as growth."

It may be added that when the early Friends experimented and developed their philosophy of education for family, meeting and school, they were creating methods and principles which have been used by succeeding generations. This has been true because they held the synoptic view of life, and because they gave children an exalted place in the Society. Many of their ideas have great value for the education of children today.

THE EPISTLES AND THE EDUCATION OF CHILDREN

THE MOST RELIABLE sources on the Friends' philosophy of education, during the early period, are found in the epistles issued each year by London Yearly Meeting. Between the years of 1659 and 1737 the epistles contain seventy-five statements in regard to the education of children. Practically every year, in their official statement, the London Yearly Meeting gave advice to Friends in regard to the education of their children. The frequency of these advices shows the important place given to the education of children.

All education was fundamentally and primarily religious. Friends did not separate education into two parts—secular and religious. They conceived of education as a unity. There was one education and it included several different types.

The Friends believed that the education of children was the task of the meeting. By the side of nearly every local meeting house was a school. There was no apology for religion, nor was it omitted from the curriculum. Religious instruction was a part of the daily program, but more than that, a religious atmosphere pervaded the entire situation.

The epistles contain more advices for instruction in religion than for any other phase of education.[8] This religious instruction was not merely for the purpose of giving information about religion, but in addition to this there was the desire that the ideals taught might be applied in practical, everyday living. This viewpoint is clearly shown in the Epistle of 1706:

> Parents should have a concern for the education of children, that in the tender years, they may be brought to a sense of God, His wisdom, power and omnipresence; and as they grow up in capacity, acquaint them with and bring them up in the frequent reading of the Scriptures of truth; to instruct them in the great love of God, through Jesus Christ, which is the work of salvation by Him, and to keep them from the fashions of the world, and in plainness of language, habit and behaviour.

Closely related to the advices on religious instruction are those which urged Friends to train their children "in such methods as Truth allows."[9] Truth, in this case, meant according to the teachings of the Society of Friends.

Very often, Friends were urged to "cause them (their children) to be frequent in reading the Holy Scriptures"[10] and to see that the children attended the meetings for worship with regularity.[11]

Friends had strong convictions on the necessity of practicing sim-

---

8. For advice on instruction in religion see the Epistles of 1672, 1688, 1689, 1690, 1695, 1700, 1701, 1709, 1710, 1712, 1715, 1718, 1719, 1723, 1730, 1732, 1733, 1734, and 1735.
9. Epistle of 1691. Also see Epistles of 1690, 1695, 1696, 1700, 1708, 1710, 1715, 1717, 1731, 1732, 1734 and 1736.
10. Epistles of 1706, 1709, 1712, 1718, 1720, 1730, 1732, 1734 and 1736.
11. Epistles of 1723, 1729 and 1737.

plicity in dress, habits and speech. They urged their children "to keep away from the vain fashions and customs of the world."[12]

The Friends were advised to train their children in some useful employment. This suggestion was made to all people no matter what the financial or social status of the family might be. The Epistle of 1703 suggests that:

> Friends of all degrees, should take due care to breed up their children in some useful and necessary employments.

But more significant than providing the situation where Friends' children might be educated "according to Truth" is the fact that the elders were to be "examples in habit and speech, and to bear the ancient testimonies of Friends."[13]

TYPES OF EDUCATION

Education in Religion

THERE was one religion, therefore one religious education—for children and adults alike. There was nothing similar to a graded course of study or organization. As previously shown, the children shared as fully as they were able in the religion of the adults. Therefore a particular education in religion, based upon the capacities and needs and interests of children, was not found among the early Friends.

It has been shown that religion was the fundamental, underlying principle of all education. The early Friends' religion was a way of life. They were greatly concerned with the immediate problems of everyday living. Therefore, education in religion was both spiritual and practical. It was spiritual because it led to some meditation and final reliance upon the Inner Light. It was practical because it led to some definite, necessary activity. Children were taught those religious ideals which would help them live their lives in the society which was theirs. The Friends also believed that religion was a personal experience. The children were warned not to rest in the faith and hope of their parents, but they themselves were expected to know religion "experimentally." For this reason the early Friends hesitated about trying to teach the children anything about religion.

---

12. Epistles of 1689, 1690, 1692, 1697, 1700, 1701, 1706, 1708, 1709, 1717, 1730, 1733, 1734, and 1735.
13. Epistles of 1692, 1693, 1708, 1712, 1719, 1729 and 1731.

This, they were to experience through the guidance of the Light Within.

Children went to meetings with their parents, and sat in silence, waiting for the voice of God. While the adults were often moved to give a verbal prayer or testimony, the children were there as listeners, and were being educated in the beliefs and ways of the Society. God was worshipped "in spirit and in truth." Even baptism and communion were spiritual, for physical elements such as water, bread and wine were considered unnecessary in the approach to God.

Children were taught to obey the voice of God. They were told that within them was something which would help them do the right, and turn away from evil. This Light Within they were to follow every day, in every phase of life.

George Fox outlined the Friends' views on education in religion, when he said:[14]

Train up all your children in the fear of God, in His new covenant of light and grace, that they may know Christ . . . and tell them from whence you have all these good things, that they may come to receive all of these good things which you receive from God and Christ, the treasure of wisdom and knowledge, that you may say that the children of your children are the crown of your old men in the Truth.

When the child asked questions about God, the parents could expect to find help for their answers through the Inner Light. Both children and parents had the capacity of following the directions of the Light. When the child would ask his parents about the nature of God, what He was, where He lived, and if one could see Him in the dark, the parents were not to evade the questions, nor tell the 'child that he was too young to know now, and he would find out later. Rather the parents were to answer to the best of their ability, and call upon God for help. They would tell the child that "God is a Spirit," and that a portion of His Spirit dwells in every person. The children would be told that God was their loving Father, their Guide and Helper.

A part of the religious education of children was a knowledge of and faith in Jesus Christ. Children were taught that Jesus was the Son of God, and that He was One with God. They were taught of the "divine nature in Christ Jesus,"[15] and that a knowledge of the love

---

14. Tuke, Samuel, Selections from the Epistles of George Fox, page 71.
15. Epistles, Volume I, Epistle of 1715, page 137.

of God could come through Jesus Christ,[16] who is the "only Mediator." Jesus was presented as the Great Example and all were urged to "diligently follow Him."[17]

The most definite statement in regard to the nature of Jesus, and that which was taught to the children, is found in the Epistle of 1732:

> That they (parents) excite them (children) to the diligent reading of those sacred writings, which plainly set forth the miraculous conception, birth, holy life, wonderful works, blessed example, meritorious death, and glorious resurrection, ascension and mediation of our Lord and Saviour Jesus Christ; and to educate their children in the belief of those important truths, as well as the belief of the inward manifestation and operation of the Spirit of God on their own minds.

Communion with God was possible for the children. This, too, was the result of waiting before God and listening to the Voice Within. The Quaker child, from babyhood, witnessed silent worship. It was a definite and frequent part of his family and meeting experiences.

In writing on the subject of children's prayer, Isaac Penington said:[18]

> Now the breathing of the child to the Father from the sense of wants for his supply, that is prayer . . . And he that begetteth the child teacheth him to pray, even by the same spirit which begat him. In watching daily to the spirit, the child is kept sensible of the will of the Father, and in His light, he sees the way wherein he is to walk. This is the living prayer of the living child, which consists not in a form of words, either read out of a book, or conceived in the mind, but in the breath of its nature issuing out from the principle of life in it to the living spring, which is the father of it.

Again he wrote:[19]

> As for praying, they will not need to be taught that outwardly; but if a true sense be kindled in them though ever so young, from that sense will arise breathings to Him that begat it, suitable to their state; which will cause growth and increase of the sense and life in them.

This attitude is typical of that accepted by the early Friends. They hesitated to give definite instruction in religion, but waited for the child to experience it by following the Light Within.

Another important part of education in religion was the instruction in and use of the Bible. Frequently, Friends were reminded,

---

16. Ibid., Epistle of 1706, page 115.
17. Ibid., Epistle of 1715, page 138.
18. Penington, Isaac, Works, Volume 2, page 109.
19. Ibid., Volume 1, page 507.

through the epistles, advices and writings of the early leaders, to bring up their children in the reading of the Scriptures. Education in religion depended greatly upon the teachings of the Bible.

Also holding an important place in the education of children were the history, faith and practice of the Friends. The first fifty years of the Society were formative years, but they came to be the sources of information and study for succeeding generations. From the earliest days of the Society, records were kept in the monthly, quarterly and yearly meetings, and these served as source materials for the writers and students of Friends' history. In addition, the journals of early Friends were written and became the study books for children. In this way the children received a knowledge of the history and beliefs of the Society. Before the end of the seventeenth century George Fox, Robert Barclay, Francis Howgill, Edward Burrough, James Nayler, Isaac Penington and other early leaders had died. Through their writings valuable materials were available for a thorough study of the Society of Friends, and the religious education of children.

Education in Morals

IN THE THOUGHT and practice of the early Friends, morality and religion belonged together. The Friends believed that moral living was the natural companion and result of religion. It was in the moral realm that many of the religious beliefs were applied.

The early writers among the Friends, had much to say concerning the morality of children. Parents were urged to teach their children, both by precept and example, the highest rules for daily living. It is a significant fact that while Friends based their doctrines upon the Inner Light, a mystical and spiritual element, yet they were very practical and established definite standards of conduct, which were directed by the revelations received through the Light.

By morals is meant the Friends' conception of right and wrong. The early Friends had certain characteristics and beliefs which distinguished them from other people. For these they were often persecuted by rebukes, beatings, imprisonments and even death. Robert Barclay called these characteristics "singular things," and discussed them under six propositions:[20]

---

20. Barclay, Robert, Apology, page 526.
   For Barclay's complete treatment of the subject, see the Apology, Proposition XV, "Salutations and Recreations."

1. That it is not lawful to give to any man such flattering titles as: Your Holiness, Your Majesty, Your Eminency, Your Excellency, Your Grace, Your Lordship, Your Honour, etc., nor use flattering words called compliments.

2. That it is not lawful for Christians to kneel, or prostrate themselves to any man, or to bow the body, or to uncover the head to him.

3. That it is not lawful to use games, sports, plays, nor among other things comedies among Christians, under the notion of recreations, which do not agree with Christian silence, gravity and sobriety; for laughing, sporting, gaming, mocking, jesting, vain talking, etc., is not Christian liberty, nor harmless mirth.

4. That it is not lawful for a Christian to use superfluities in apparel, as are of no use, save for ornament and vanity.

5. That it is not lawful for Christians to swear at all, under the Gospel, not only vainly and in common discourse, which was also forbidden under the Mosaical law, but even not in judgment before the magistrate.

6. That it is not lawful for Christians to resist evil or to war or fight in any case.

Barclay continued by denouncing games, sports, plays, cards, dice, dance and singing. He strongly condemned oaths, revenge, war, fightings and called them "the fashions and lusts of the world."

Barclay believed that the Inner Light would help children to know the right from wrong. He held that if children obeyed the directions of the Light, they would know how to overcome and refrain from those recreations which seemed to him to be so un-Christian.

There was, however, a positive side to Barclay's standards of morality. He believed that there were "innocent divertisements which may sufficiently serve for relaxation of the mind, such as: [21]

Friends to visit one another; to hear or read history; to speak soberly of the present or past transactions; to follow after gardening; to use geometrical and mathematical experiments.

In his statements about recreations and particularly in his ideas about "innocent divertisements," Barclay gave no evidence of differences between children and adults, and suggested methods of little interest to children. He seemed to think of both, entirely on the same level.

The primary principle of morality, according to Barclay, was to relax the mind in keeping with the will of God, and to please, honor and love Him. Any and all recreations were to be "done to the glory of God," and anything contrary to that was considered as immoral.

---

21. Barclay, Robert, Apology, page 500.

The great objection to games, sports, plays, dancing and the like was the belief that they would draw people away from God. It was feared that they would lead people into lust, vanity and wantonness.

George Fox stated his own attitude toward all moral questions, and the basis of living above the evil, and desire to do good, when he answered the problem of war. On this subject, he said: [22]

I told them . . . that I lived in the virtue of that life and power that took away the occasion of all wars.

Fox seemed to live above or beyond the need of the vanities and "un-Christian" practices of the world in which he lived. In his teaching and by his example, Fox gave instruction in the good life. He urged Friends so to live that the world would know, taking their lives as examples, that they lived fairly and honestly. He declared that Friends became well known for their faithfulness and that they kept their word in their dealings and: [23] "if a child were sent to their shops for anything, he was as well used as his parents would have been."

The best illustration of the nature of moral education is found in the epistles. These show that the principle of morality, as taught by the Friends, included: modesty, plainness, simplicity and sobriety in apparel, habits and language. The teachers and parents were urged to keep the children "out of everything that would corrupt their manners." Children were taught to keep out of the "vain fashions and corrupt customs of the world."

Throughout the epistles, the early Friends questioned any act of life which might detract from that which they called true Christianity. They had much to say about the recreations of their day. They disapproved of and taught against most of the amusements and recreations of their time. Parents were asked to keep their children from the ways of the world with its corrupt language, manners, vain and needless things in apparel, buildings, furniture and houses. Children were to refrain from all immodest and indecent actions. They were to dress and act in keeping with the Friends' moral standards of simplicity and [24] usefulness. In all of this, parents were to be good and worthy examples to their children, and to correct them when it was necessary. In this connection, George Fox said: [25]

---

22. Fox, George, Autobiography, page 128.
23. Ibid., page 198.
24. Epistle of 1709.

And all Friends in the wisdom of God train up your children in the fear of God, that they may receive the wisdom of God: and as they are able, they may be instructed and kept employed in some lawful calling. . . . And see that your children are trained up in soberness, and holiness, and righteousness and temperance and meekness and gentleness and lowliness and modesty in their apparel and carriage, and so to exhort your children and families in the Truth, that the Lord may be glorified in your families. And teach your children when they are young, then will they remember it when they are old, according to Solomon's counsel, so that your children may be a blessing to you and not a curse.

As early as 1689, George Whitehead, the Friends' missionary of religious liberty, was greatly grieved with the "scandal" as practiced by the children of Friends.[26] He regretted that the children were "degenerating into pride, and height of spirit and apparel," and were "imitating the world." Perhaps as he was preaching a longer sermon than usual, some of the children had become restless and seemed to take no interest in the good advice he was giving. Or probably, one of the girls had a ribbon in her hair, or her gown may have been white, rather than the somber gray; or some boy may have dared to wear a red necktie which his uncle had sent from London, or perhaps he had been so disrespectful as to have said "you" to one person. At any rate, this devout leader was greatly concerned with the manner in which young Friends acted and in the way they had forsaken the Truth and had followed the world.

One of the practices, which the Friends believed carried great moral significance, was the use of the plain language. Many of the epistles and advices warn parents to see that their children do not use the world's language, but always use the plain and simple one. George Fox believed that the Lord had directed him to use thee and thou. Of this he wrote: [27]

I was required to thee and thou all men and women, without any respect to rich or poor, great or small.

Since this opening came to George Fox from God, he practiced it without question. He taught the same to his followers, and they taught it to their children. For centuries, the plain language has been practiced by Friends.

The best treatment in regard to the reasons for the use of the plain

25. Fox, George, Works, Volume 7, page 345.
26. Tuke, Samuel, Memoir of George Whitehead, page 159.
27. Fox, George, Autobiography, page 105.

language, in addition to the divine opening, is given in a rare book entitled, "A Battle-Door for Teachers and Professors to Learn Singular and Plural." George Fox suggested to John Stubbs and Benjamin Furly that the book be written, and he himself "added some things to it." The purpose of the book was to show that thee and thou were proper and the usual form of speech when addressing one person. The Scriptures and books in thirty different languages were used to prove the validity of the belief. The book convinced King Charles that the plain language was correct.

Education in morals was a definite part of the program of education for children. It grew out of a deep religious concern and desire to apply the ideals of Christianity to the affairs of life. Children as well as adults were admonished to put these ideals into daily practice.

Secular Education

THE THIRD TYPE of education, among the early Friends is that which is usually called secular education. It was the common practice in the Society for each monthly meeting to have a school for the education of Friends' children. These early schools seldom went beyond the elementary grades.

Throughout the epistles, advices and journals, parents were urged to see that their children were trained "in useful and necessary learning," and "in the common branches of learning." The subjects taught were those usually offered in elementary grades. The children were given instruction in reading, writing, spelling, penmanship, grammar, geography, mathematics and elementary science. The Quakers objected so strenuously to "heathen authors" that foreign languages were given little place, although Greek and Latin were offered.

John Bellers, in his "Proposals for a College of Industry" defined the Quaker views of education in rudimentary knowledge.[28] He said that "beyond reading and writing, further learning will not be so useful." In this connection he was, no doubt, thinking of the simple life as recommended by Friends in their education in religion and morals. Bellers made the plea that the children should not be given absolute freedom in the educational process, but they should be given definite direction and supervision. He believed that secular education could be taught best by an application to practical employment.

---

28. Bellers, John, Proposals for a College of Industry (1695), pages 15-17.

He thought that any "silly employ" was an enemy to education and to the children. He held that children could and should be kept at something usually of value to them, and that "besides reading, boys and girls might be taught to knit and spin, ... turning, etc." He believed that education "should be seasoned with religious lessons from the Scriptures."

In the seventeenth century, this Quaker educator implied that education should be "life-centered," and that to be successful, it must be "activity leading to further activity." He advocated freedom with proper supervision. He also showed the place of religion in the educational process.

Secular education, as well as all other types, was under the direction of the meeting and was motivated by a religious concern. It was education for practical use.

Education in Manual Arts

ANOTHER type of training, among the early Friends, was education in manual arts. By this term is meant useful skills or trades. The Friends believed that idleness on the part of any people, and especially among children was a great danger, and that education, therefore, should include something useful to the individual and society.

The Friends believed that religion should direct all life, therefore, it should guide the educational process. Quakerism was a religion which called for a life of simplicity. Friends were urged to live on a scale of well-regulated economy. In 1686, George Fox recommended to the Friends: [29]

That you may all study to be approved of God, in innocency, virtue, simplicity, and faithfulness; and so labouring and studying to be quiet in the will of God, in all conditions. And whatsoever ye do in word or deed, do all in the name of the Lord Jesus.

The testimonies of the Society of Friends influenced education in manual arts in two ways. They ruled Friends out of certain callings, such as the army, law, politics, priesthood and university teaching. On the other hand, they led Friends into the study and practice of the more simple employments such as farming, store-keeping, industry and manufacturing. About the only profession open to Friends was the practice of medicine. The Friends' ministers were "called of God," and were trained by the leading of the Inner Light, so formal

29. Epistles, Volume I, pages 29-30, Statement by George Fox.

training for the ministry did not find a place in the educational system of the Friends.

The attitude of Friends toward education in manual arts was given by George Fox, when he said: [30]

And all Friends in the wisdom of God train up your children in the fear of God, that they may receive wisdom of God; and and as they are capable, they may be instructed and kept employed in some lawful calling, that they may be diligent, serving the Lord in the things that are good: that none may live idle, and be destroyers of the creation, and thereby become burdensome to others, and to the just in themselves; but that in the wisdom of God all may walk and with it all things may be ordered.

In a more general way Fox defined this type of education when he recommended the establishment of schools for teaching children: "Whatsoever things were civil and useful."[31] This statement of Fox directed all education in manual arts among the early Friends.

The second principle in regard to education in manual arts was the belief that all children, both of the rich and of the poor should be taught some useful trade. All children, regardless of position, were to be instructed in some worthy trade.

The Epistle of 1709 gave the following advice:

That the children of both the rich and the poor may early be provided with industrious employments, that they may not grow up in idleness, looseness and vice.

John Bellers urged the practical education of both rich and poor, when he said: [32]

Children of estates may be boarded and educated in all useful learning, who seeing others work, at spare times instead of playing would be learning some trade, work not being more labour than play; and seeing others work to imitate them would be as much diversion to the children as play, which would the more inure them to business when grown up, the plant who through the want of which hath ruined many, who will be doing if not of good, of evil; and idle learning being little better than the learning of idleness.

In his book, "Proposals for a college of Industry," John Bellers listed forty-six trades which he suggested in his training course. These callings, he thought, were in keeping with the religious faith of the Friends, and he desired that Friends' children should receive such practical training. The following is the list of trades suggested by

---

30. Fox, George, Works, Volume 7, page 345.
31. Fox, George, Autobiography, page 461.
32. Bellers, John, Proposals for a College of Industry, page 11.

Mr. Bellers, and his spelling is used in the list:[33] shoe-makers, brewers, barbers, linnen weavers, gardiners, tallow-chandlers, cappers, taylors, butchers, physitians, woollen weavers, felmongers, soap-makers, carpenters, bakers, upholsters, cooks, tanners, thred-makers, hatters, joyners, coopers, pin-makers, store-keepers, linnen spinners and carders, bed-makers, sempsters to make and mend clothes, plow-men, shepherds, flax-dressors, smiths, needle-makers, nurses, woollen spinners and carders, washers, knitters or weavers of stockins, plow-boys, ledgers, bricklayers and labourers, butlers, spinners and carders for stockins, dairy-maids, house-cleaners, hinds for cattle, taskers, labourers.

George Fox gave a list, much smaller than that of Bellers, for apprenticeship for children. All the ones given by Fox are included in the above list, but Fox added: masons, wheelwrights, ploughwrights, curriers, and nailers.

The System of Apprenticeship

ANOTHER interest of Friends which was a part of the education in manual arts was the system of apprenticeship. This system developed in England as a part of the child labour methods and is mentioned as early as the thirteenth century. By 1450 apprenticeship was practiced by most of the guilds. The Statute of Artificers, passed in 1562, made apprenticeship a necessity for all who wished to enter crafts, industries, and trades. This law was in force until 1814.

Both boys and girls were apprenticed. The ages when the children were taken and the number of years required in service as apprentice varied in localities and in guilds. The average age was ten years, and the time of service usually seven years. In some instances children were taken as young as three years of age, and were required to serve as long as ten years.

The chief purpose of the system of apprenticeship was technical training in a definite craft or industry. Children were apprenticed to a tradesman who agreed to train them in his particular trade. At the close of time of service the apprentices were supposed to be ready to enter their selected fields of labour. The apprentices were considered as members of the master's family, and they were expected to serve him faithfully.

The master had obligations other than training the child for a

33. Ibid, pages 5-6.

given trade. He entered into a contract with the parents or guardians of the child, and stated the definite conditions under which the apprentice was taken. The guilds outlined the requirements and made regular inspections to see that the contract was fulfilled. Either the apprentice, parents or master could appeal to the guild in case of difficulty or controversy. Usually the master was expected to furnish the apprentice food, lodging, clothing and provide for his physical needs. In most cases, the master had to provide secular education, probably all the formal instruction which an apprentice received. This seldom consisted of more than elementary arts such as arithmetic, reading and writing. In the event that the apprentice would need a foreign language in his trade, the master was required to provide such instruction. In some places the master was required to take the children to church and to see that they attended family worship. During the apprenticeship, children formed their characters, received training for adult life and citizenship, and developed their capacities and skills. The master stood "in loco parentis." He was supposed to see that the apprentice received the proper education in a trade, morals, secular subjects and often in religion.

The poor law of 1601 ordered the justices of the peace to bind out as apprentices the children of poor parents who could not support the family. Later this system served as the method of providing for orphan and pauper children. This often led to ill treatment which was akin to slavery.

By 1645 the apprenticeship system was on the decline on account of the Civil War. After the restoration of Charles II the system was revived although the guilds had great difficulty in attempting to enforce the rules. This was the condition of the system during the early period of Quakerism.

On account of their religious belief, the children of Friends were not permitted to enroll as apprentices. Because the children of Friends were disqualified to serve as apprentices, and on account of the Friends' principles of the care of the poor and guarded education, the Quakers found it necessary to have a deep concern for the system as it related to their own children. For these reasons they took particular interest in apprenticeship and adopted definite rules for it.

Among the Friends, families were requested to select with great care the places where their children were to serve their apprenticeship. As much as possible, they were to place their children in the families of Friends. Basic in the interest of Friends in the system of apprenticeship was the concern of the welfare of the children. In the system as it was generally practiced in England, Friends saw the demoralizing nature of the method. Often children were terribly mistreated, their physical needs were neglected and the moral and spiritual influences were exceedingly unwholesome.

The Friends were interested in training children in some useful, worthy trade in keeping with the profession of the Society, and at the same time in giving the children adequate instruction and ample opportunities for experience in religion. The Friends' religion was closely related to morality, and therefore, the apprentices were expected to be given proper moral training. Apprentices were expected to attend both family and meeting worship.

Four principles determined the nature of apprenticeship for children: trades which parents might desire for their children; trades to which children were most inclinable; the opportunities for children in such trades; and the character of the person to whom the children were to be apprenticed.

George Fox sanctioned the system of apprenticeship and gave definite instructions in regard to the matter. He outlined methods to be followed by the local monthly meetings. He wrote:[34]

Know all Friends that are poor, widows, or others that have children fit to put out to apprenticeship; so that once a quarter you may set forth an apprentice in your quarterly meeting; so you may set forth four in a year, in each county, or more if there be occasion. This apprentice, when out of his time, may help his father or mother, and support the family that is decayed; and in so doing all may come to live comfortably. This being done in your quarterly meetings, you will have knowledge throughout the county, in the monthly and particular meetings, of masters who are fit for them; and of such trades as their parents or you desire, or the children are most inclinable to. Thus being placed out to Friends, they may be trained up in Truth; and by this means in the wisdom of God, you may preserve Friends' children in the Truth, and nursers and preservers of their relations in the ancient days.

A very excellent advice for all children as well for apprentices, was given by Edward Burrough, when he said:[35]

And all ye apprentices, learn ye the fear of the Lord, and take heed of temptations, lest ye be destroyed both soul and body by them; learn not to

34. Fox, George, Works, Volume 2, pages 93-94.
35. Burrough, Edward, The Memorable Works of a Son of Thunder and Consolation, page 221. For similar advice see: Friends Library, Volume 13, page 122. Also see the Epistles for 1703, 1709, 1730, 1732, 1737.

dissemble, nor to defraud, nor take not instructions how to cozen and cheat, but first seek the Kingdom of God and its righteousness. . . . Covet not after riches, neither study how to be proud and vain-glorious; give not yourselves to craft and human policies nor to deceive any people, but fear God and keep his commandments and be subject to your masters and obey them in all things that are good.

MATERIALS OF EDUCATION

The Place of the Bible

THE BIBLE held a place of first importance among the materials used by the Friends in education. It was not considered a final authority, in neither education nor religion; only the guidance of God through the Inner Light was that. However, the Friends believed that the directions of the Inner Light were in keeping with Scriptural teachings. George Fox went so far as to say that even his divine openings were verified by the Bible.[36] The Friends turned to the Bible for proof of their doctrines and for their standards of morality. Since it held such an important part in the thought and life of the early Friends, it was considered the best and most essential material to be used in the educational process.

Friends were advised by epistles, journals and sermons to be "diligent in reading of Scripture in the families." They were to see that the children, also, read the Bible frequently. They were to be guided by the admonitions and teachings of the Scriptures.

It was the duty of teachers to give opportunity for the reading and studying of the Bible, so that the children might become well acquainted with the various portions of it. The children were taught that they would be blessed in the study and practice of the scriptural truths. Children were not to have books which taught against or were inconsistent with the Bible, and parents and teachers were warned to keep such books away from children. The Bible was supreme, above all books.

The Bible was very often used by the ministers of the Society. As the children attended meetings, and as they listened to the sermons, they heard stories and passages from the Bible.[37] In the home and

---

36. Fox, George, Autobiography, page 103.
37. See Norman Penney, The First Publishers of Truth, pages 14, 18, 34, 62, 116, 128, 135, 139, 143, 145, 238, 244, 256, 286, 292, 302, 336, 364, etc., for the use of the Bible by the early ministers of the Society.

school it was used in the worship. This book became a part of the children's religious instruction and experience.

There is no evidence of "selected" or graded Bible study, during the time of the early Friends. For the family worship, the parents selected those portions of Scripture which they felt should be used. There was the general attitude that any and all parts of the Bible were suitable for all ages, children and adults alike. The portions recommended for children were most inclusive. Practically the entire Bible was used. Biblical history, poetry, prophecy, stories and letters found place in the religious educational process. In sermons and epistles references were made to these sections, as well as to the outstanding personalities of the Bible. The great characters were presented to the children as heroes. In this way, Friends' children had a rather thorough and inclusive study of the Bible.

William Penn in his "Advice to Children," wrote:[38]

> I would suggest that you read the Scriptures daily; the Old Testament for history, chiefly; the Psalms for meditation and devotion; the prophets for comfort and hope; but especially the New Testament for doctrine, faith and worship.

Barclay's Apology is the best authority for the place of the Bible among the early Friends.[39] He believed that the Scriptures were "the most excellent writings in the world" and that they should hold the highest place among all books. But, true to his belief that the Inner Light was the chief doctrine of Christianity, he held that the Bible was a "secondary rule," and should be subordinate to the Light or Spirit. He thought that the Bible should be studied and used according to the guidance of the Light. Just as the Scripture confirmed the revelations of the Light, the Light was the final authority in finding the truth of the Scripture.

In his book written for the instruction of children, and entitled "A Catechism and Confession of Faith," Barclay gives in detail the faith of Friends in the form of question and answer. In the Catechism the answers to the questions are quoted from the Bible. In the confession of Faith the statements are, for the most part, quotations from the Bible. The following are given as examples of the questions and the answers which tell of the nature and value of the Scriptures: [40]

---

38. Penn, William, Select Works (London 1771), page 847.
39. For Barclay's complete treatment, "Concerning the Scriptures," see the Apology, Proposition III, pages 72-97.
40. Barclay, Robert, A Catechism and a Confession of Faith, pages 3-6.

Question: For what end were the Scriptures written?

Answer: For whatsoever things were written aforetime, were written for our learning, that we, through patience and comfort of the Scriptures, might have hope. (Romans 15:4)

Question: For what are they profitable?

Answer: Thou hast known the Holy Scriptures, which are able to make thee wise unto salvation through faith which is in Christ Jesus. All Scripture is given by inspiration of God and is profitable for doctrine, for reproof, for correction, for instruction in righteousness that the man of God may be perfect, thoroughly furnished unto all good works. (2 Timothy 3:15-17)

Question: The Scriptures are, then, to be regarded because they came from the Spirit, and they also testify that not they, but the Spirit is to lead into all truth. In what respect doth Christ command to search them?

Answer: Ye search the Scriptures, for in them ye think ye have eternal life, and they are they which testify of me. (John 5:39)

George Fox agreed with Robert Barclay in the belief that the Scriptures were second to the Inner Light in authority. He believed that the Bible was given by the revelation and inspiration of God, and that it must be interpreted by this same Spirit. To interpret the Scriptures the individual must seek guidance from the Light Within. In his letter to the governor of the Barbadoes, Fox clearly set forth the Friends' attitudes toward the Scriptures, in a statement which is used, even to the present time, by most bodies of Friends. The abstract is direct and leaves no uncertainty as to the position of Friends on the nature and use of the Bible:[41]

Concerning the Holy Scriptures: we believe they were given forth by the Holy Spirit of God through the Holy men of God, who, as the Scripture itself declares (2 Peter 1:21) spoke as they were moved of the Holy Ghost. We believe they are to be read, believed, and fulfilled and that they are profitable for doctrine, for reproof, for correction, and for instruction in righteousness that the man of God may be perfect, thoroughly furnished unto all good works, and are able to make wise unto salvation, through faith in Christ Jesus.

But the use of the Bible by George Fox is even more significant than what he said about it. His sermons, advices, letters and journal and all his writings show a great knowledge of and dependence upon the Scriptures. He constantly refers to the Bible and suggests its use in the process of education. It was said of Fox that he had an unusual gift in opening the Scriptures and that his instructions were most helpful to all who heard him. The example of George Fox no doubt

---

41. Discipline of the Five Years Meeting (1930), page 14.

had great influence upon families, and particularly upon children. They would hear him preach, would see him use the Bible, and would conclude that it was the desirable thing to do.

William Penn thought that not only were the men inspired who wrote the Bible, but that the Bible was the "declaratory word of God." He urged the frequent use of the Bible in the family and by children.

Isaac Penington also, placed much authority in the Bible. He believed that the purpose of Biblical study was to turn the people to the Light. He felt that the Bible contained messages from God to mankind, and that the way of life, according to Christ, was explained in the Scriptures. Penington thought that the Bible could reach the several states of men, and could be of great value to children.

One of the early Quaker preachers believed that he was called to turn people to the Scriptures. He exhorted parents to teach them to their children, for he thought that the Bible could speak to the needs of children as well as to those of adults.

A personal testimony as to the value of the reading of the Bible during childhood, and its effect upon later life is given by George Whitehead. His attitude toward the Bible was in line with that held by other early Friends. He testified that there was considerable advantage to him in the reading of the Scriptures, although he could not understand all of which he read. He said that it was a great help to his "secret meditations." He urged parents to have their children read the Scriptures frequently. He wrote: [42]

I have sometimes observed pretty innocent children in reading in the Bible effected with the good things they have read, from a secret belief in them, which hath had such impressions on their memories and affections, that they have been induced to a more serious consideration thereof, when the Lord has opened their understandings in some measure by the Light of His grace.

The epistles and the advices of the early Friends recommended that children should read only those books which were consistent with the Scriptures; and those which told of the Christian way of life. All books should be for the moral and religious education of children. Parents were warned not to permit their children to read improper books.

Parents were told to keep their children from reading any books that "have any tendency to prejudice the profession of the Christian

---

42. Whitehead, George, Memoirs of, pages 43-44.

religion."[43] They were to keep from their children, any books:[44]

As have any tendency to lead their minds from God, and draw the youthful affections to a love of the world, and desire after the vanities and evils that are therein . . . and prevent the children from reading such vile and corrupt books as manifestly tend to oppose and reject the divine authority of the Holy Scriptures, and to introduce Deism, Atheism, and all manner of infidelity and corruption, both in principle and practice.

The epistles clearly indicate that the early Friends believed that the Scriptures were of first and supreme importance and that they were held in highest esteem above all other books. They were to be read by the children, and no books should be given to children which taught anything contrary to the teachings of the Bible. It is clear that Friends objected to all plays, dramas, novels, "or vain and idle pamphlets."[45] Books for children should not corrupt the minds, but lead children to God. Children should read religious books, especially the Bible.

The Journals of Friends

IT WAS the custom of the early Friends to keep journals, particularly of their travels "for the Truth's sake," and their ministry and suffering in those activities. Many of these were printed during the lifetime of the individuals, while others were published soon after the decease of the writers. These journals were widely circulated and were commonly found in homes and meetings. They were given to the children in order that they might become acquainted with the founders and leaders of the Society. Much of the history, experiences, faith and the practice of the founders of the Society were contained in these writings. They became a part of the educational material for children.

Similar materials were found in the lives and memoirs of Friends. Many of these, as well as the journals, were approved and published by London Yearly Meeting. They usually began with statements concerning the birth, education, works and death of the individual. They frequently went into considerable detail in regard to the childhood experiences, the call to religious service, the various activities pertaining to that endeavor, and the meeting's appreciation of the individual.

---

43. Epistle of 1723.
44. Epistle of 1729.
45. Epistle of 1720.

Friends' Books for Children
Published before 1737.

JOSEPH SMITH, in 1867, published "A Descriptive Catalogue of Friends' Books, or Books Written by Members of the Society of Friends, Commonly Called Quakers, From their First Rise to the Present Time, Interspersed with Critical Remarks, and Occasional Biographical Notices, and Including All Writings by Authors before Joining, and by Those after Having Left the Society, whether Adverse or Not, as Far as Known." The catalogue consists of two large volumes and a small supplement.

The list of books for children reveals some interesting facts concerning both the types of books contained and the nature of books which were not included in the number. The list contains fifty-eight books for children. The books may be divided into three groups: first, those giving advice, counsel and exhortations to children. There were thirty-two of these books. In this group is one book by William Penn, entitled, "Fruits of a Father's Love, being the Advice of William Penn to his Children." Fifty-five per cent of the books for children had to do with admonitions for the good life according to the belief of the Friends. Secondly, there were catechisms and textbooks. There were nineteen of these. George Fox wrote a catechism bearing the following title: "A Catechisme for Children, that they may come to learne of Christ the Light, the Truth, the Way that Leads to know the Father, the God of All Truth; Instructions for Right Spelling, and Plain Directions for Reading and Writing the True English. With Several Delightful Things very useful and necessary for Young and Old to Read and Learn; A Paper for Little Children—beginning with 'Christ is the Truth'." Thirty-three per cent of the books for children were for the direct purpose of instruction. Thirdly, there were books dealing with the matter of life and death. These were for the purpose of developing piety within the lives of children. There were seven of these books. An illustration of this type of book is Richard Bockett's, "Fruits of Early Piety." Twelve per cent of the books for children told of the pious lives of other children and quoted their sayings in regard to death. All of the books for children quoted by Mr. Smith, had to do with the moral and religious education of the children, and indicate the sober nature of children's books.

The second fact in regard to the list of books for children is the type of books which were not included. There were no books dealing with child nature and life. There was nothing for the entertainment of children. Any books dealing with plays, romances or the working of the imagination were looked upon as "vain and worldly."

Each monthly meeting had a book committee for the purpose of passing upon books before they were published.[46] This limited the type and number of books issued by Friends. It clearly and narrowly defined the nature and contents of books. This attitude grew out of the Friends' principle of guarded education.

In the book, "The Battle-Door for Teachers and Professors to Learn Singular and Plural," the authors wrote against the "Heathen Books," such as the Roman classical writings, and urged parents and teachers to use the Bible rather than these books from the "heathen." The authors objected to getting help from the "Heathen Writers," for such taught the children "nonsense." On these matters they said: [47]

And now you that are called Christians, you must be vain to have Heathen Books to teach your children in your schools, whereby the children must learn the Heathen's words. . . . And therefore, if you will teach children other tongues, and have it translated into English, teach and translate the things of God, the Scriptures for children to learn, and not translate Heathen's work to corrupt the earth with them, but let all be burned and made an end of.

In the same book, definite criticism was made of certain textbooks used for the purpose of teaching Latin. The objections to these books were most interesting, for they not only give a criticism of the textbooks, but also show something of the principles of religion and philosophy of education as held by the early Friends. An illustration of these criticisms is given as follows:

Title of Book: "Pueriles Confabulatiunculae."

(Children's Talks.)

Objections to the book:

First, that the book used you for thou.

Second, certain translations, listed in the books, and considered as incorrect and bad examples for children. Among these were:

"My fist should have gone about your ears a good while ago."

"And I'll knock out all those teeth of his."

"Hang the school, and the master too."

"A pox take all the brewers."

"Drink lustily."

---

46. See Epistle of 1691, Epistles, Volume I, page 58.
47. The Battle-Door, pages 2-3 (at end of the book).

"Why do you stand here, your Russian rogue?"

In conclusion, the authors of the Battle-Door said:

Friends, consider this and let the book be burnt as fit for nothing but destruction, and that spirit which invented it.

The Rules of Discipline

As THE Society of Friends grew, and as organization became necessary, the Meetings for Discipline (the business meetings) were established. The first one was held in 1653. Records of such meetings have been kept since 1656. The first meeting sent out certain "directions and advices." As the meetings developed, they continued these directions and they came to be known as the Rules of Discipline.

The occasions for the establishment of such meetings were the "sufferings" of Friends, particularly those in prisons. The prisoners as well as their families were in dire need of help, and the Friends cared for them. They also gave particular attention to poor children and orphans.

As George Fox advised, the Rules of Discipline had to do with the promotion of charity and piety. Advices were given for the following topics: the care of the poor, marriage, records of birth and death, proper care of the estates and inheritances of children, honesty and integrity in business, ideals for the ministry and worship, provision for membership (including the membership of children), rules for church organization and government, the education of children and the training and care of the apprentices.

The Disciplines served, not so much as class room materials, but as aids in the development of the Friends' philosophy of education, and in this way helped in the direction of the educational processes in the family, meeting and school. The Rules of Discipline were available for the children and teachers, and were used in the study of the history and doctrine of the Society of Friends.

The Advices as Educational Material

SOME interesting and somewhat distinctive materials were known as advices. Some of these were written for parents, while others were definitely for children. They were, in many cases, published and intended for the education and use of children. They had to do with all elements of life, and were particularly concerned with the proper instruction of children in religion, morals and manual arts.

John Banks, in an advice to parents, urged them to bring up their children according to the Truth as held and practiced by Friends: [48]

You who are parents of children, train them up in the fear of the Lord, as becomes the Truth, and give no liberty to them, nor indulge them in word or action that is contrary to the truth of God. Teach them the plain language of thee and thou, to every single person, and to name the days of the week and months of the year according to the testimony of the Holy Scripture; for this is according to Truth; and not as the people of the world, after the names of the heathens' gods.

In the memoir of John Camm it is said of him, that he was a tender and godly father, and deeply concerned with the religious welfare of his family. He often called them together and exhorted them "to fear the Lord and walk in holiness of life as became the Gospel." [49]

John Crocker wrote the following advice to his children, especially to his eldest child, Charles: [50]

Remember thy Creator in the days of thy youth. The more thou comest to do this, the more the Lord will love thee. What opportunities thou hast, spend in serving God, by privately walking and meditating on the things of God, and what relates to thy eternal good. Keep to meetings, and when there bend thy mind to God. . . . Delight thyself in the company of good, honest Friends. . . . Be diligent to hear the ancient Friends. . . . Flee from all bad company. . . . Often inquire in thy heart, of God and the way towards His kingdom. . . . Watch in the light of the Lord who shineth in the secret of the soul. You should take heed unto it, for it never consenteth to any evil action; mind the leadings of it, for it always leads unto that which is good. Often commune with it in stillness, that thou mayest be more and more acquainted with it, which as it is obeyed, will open wisdom unto thee, whereby thou wilt come to be wise in the things of God.

Read not in foolish books, with which the nation abounds, but read in the Holy Scriptures in which there is a great deal of comfort. . . . Likewise read Friends' books and others which tend to edification. . . . Let not thy mind out too soon to many whilst thou art young, but rather tarry until the years of twenty-five or thirty. . . . And God, if sought unto, will so direct thee that thou mayest have a wife who is suitable for thee, and helpful to thee in all conditions both spiritual and temporal; for therein consisteth the great joy of married life. Choose one who cometh of good stock . . . whose words are few and savoury. Choose not by the eye as to beauty, nor for the abundance she may have of this world. . . . But let the eye be to the better part. . . . Love her and cherish her, as becomes a faithful husband.

In writing of the education of Friends' children, William Ed-

48. Friends Library, Volume 2, page 53, Journal of John Banks.
49. Ibid., Volume 5, page 475.
50. Ibid., Volume 14, pages 12-13.

mundson disapproved of schools which were not maintained by the Society:[51]

Experience has taught us that in sending children to schools where books are used filled with idle stories, lying wonders, and invented ceremonies, besides evil conversations both in words and actions, being countenanced if not encouraged by too many school-masters and mistresses, childish nature in youth is prone to listen thereto, rather than to things that tend to virtue and sobriety, and being grafted in their minds when young, grow up with them, and so obstruct better things that tend to godliness and their salvation.

A very long, but interesting and practical "advice to children" was given by William Penn.[52] In this advice William Penn gave principles of living which have universal and lasting value. His ideals are consistent with not only early Friends' but modern philosophy of education and morality.

William Penn began by saying that: "all true wisdom and happiness is the holy fear of God," and this happiness, believed Penn, was revealed to the individual through the Light Within.

He concludes by giving an advice which sounds very modern. He says:

"If God give you children, love them with wisdom, correct them with affection. Never strike in passion, and suit the correction to the age as well as the fault. Punish them more by understanding than the rod, and shew them the folly, shame and undutifulness of their faults; rather than an angry countenance shew a grieved one, and you will sooner affect their natures, and with a nobler sense than a servile and rude chastisement can produce. . . . Pride and vain glory both should be avoided in the religious education of youth.

AGENCIES AND METHODS OF EDUCATION

FOR THE achievement of the aims of the various types of education, there were three agencies: the family, the meeting and the school. These three institutions were guided by the Friends' philosophy of education. Much of the same material, and many of the same methods were used in each of them. This is an expression of the synoptic view of life. The agencies were organized for the purpose of developing complete, Christian personalities. Religion guided the educational process in family, meeting and school.

---

51. Friends Library, Volume 2, page 157.
52. For complete advice see: Penn, William, "Select Works" (London 1771), pages 847-862.

The Family as an Educational Agency

THE EARLY Friends believed that the primary responsibility for the education of children rested upon the parents. The Friends believed that the education of children was a Christian duty and opportunity, and that the family should serve as the chief educational agency.[53]

A typical illustration of the advices given in the epistles is the one issued in 1688. It is as follows:

> We do intreat and desire that parents and governors of families, that ye diligently lay to heart your work and concern in your generation for the Lord, and the charge committed to you; not only in becoming good examples unto the younger sort, but also to use your power in your own families in educating your children and servants in modesty, sobriety, and in the fear of God, curbing the extravagant humour in the young ones . . . and when you see a libertine, wanton spirit appear in your children and servants, that lusteth after the vain customs and fashions of the world, either in dressings, habits or outward adornings, . . . then look to yourselves and discharge your trust for God, and for the good of their souls, exhorting in meekness and commanding in wisdom.

George Fox, who had the education of children at heart as much as any other early Friend, and who continually expressed a great desire that parents should make adequate provision for it, said:[54]

> So now they (children) come to be exercised in the grace of God, and to admonish and exhort, reprove and rebuke, and to keep all the family modest, honest, virtuous, sober and civil, and not to give liberty, nor indulge that which tends to vice or lasciviousness, or any evil, or idleness, or slothfulness, or the fashions of the world, which pass away; and to stop all vain words and idle talking and stories and tales which are unprofitable; but rather turn their ears to godliness which they should be trained up and exercised in; . . . And if either men or women suffer such things they suffer that which defiles their children and families; and therefore, such things are to be reproved in families, and the children to be stopped from going into such things.

Education in the family had little to do with the learning of secular subjects, but it was greatly interested in the religious, moral and practical education of children. No doubt much of the instruction was indirect, and Friends lived without particular awareness of the

---

53. Epistles containing requests that parents should provide proper education for their children were issued in the following years: 1688, 1689, 1691, 1692, 1693, 1695, 1696, 1700, 1701, 1703, 1706, 1708, 1709, 1710, 1712, 1713, 1715, 1717, 1718, 1719, 1720, 1723, 1730, 1731, 1732, 1733, 1734, 1735, 1736, and 1737.
54. Fox, George, Works, Volume 8, page 95.

fact that the educational process was going on, but nevertheless the children were being educated.

The Friends thought that the education of children was a responsibility given to them by the Lord, and that they would be held accountable for this charge. They undertook the task as a holy, spiritual obligation. Their primary object was to bring up the children "in the fear of the Lord," according to the Truth as held by the Society.

One of the greatest religious educational agencies in the family was worship. In practicing silence, reading the Bible, and in hearing the prayers and testimonies of parents and visiting Friends, the children were led to definite religious experiences. The same type of worship was followed in the family as in the meeting. If Friends lived so far away from the meeting house that regular attendance was impossible, they were advised to "keep meetings in your families, to wait upon God," and in this way the children were trained in worship which led to a knowledge of God.

Education in the family also required training in morals. Friends' children were taught honesty, modesty and sobriety. They were kept away from the evil and extravagant customs and manners of the world. They were to refrain from idle conversation and questionable associates. They were to develop moral standards by a moral participation in the life of the family and the community. In the moral realms they were to apply that which they had learned in their religious education.

Education in a Friends' family was very practical. The children were guarded against idleness and slothfulness. All were trained in the useful employments usually found within a family group. All shared in the responsibilities and opportunities of the home and for the means of a livelihood such as the farm or store.

The Quaker boy was held responsible for a full wood box and a full water supply. It was his task to bring the horses and the cattle from the fields. He gathered the fruit and the vegetables. As he became older, he shared more fully in the duties about the farm. While the boy was thus engaged, his sister helped in the house. There were dishes to wash, fires to make, and babies to watch. As she grew, the girl took more and more of the responsibilities in the duties of a well-regulated family.[55]

---

55. For a beautiful and interesting story of family life among the Quakers, see:
Robert Dudley, "In My Youth," Bobbs-Merrill Company (1914).
Other stories of family life are found in: Rufus M. Jones, "Finding the Trail

In the process of education in the family the father and mother shared in the task of training the children. The father trained the boys in the work out-of-doors, while the mother managed the instruction of the girls in the house. By formal instruction and practical example the parents inspired the children to a thorough education in religion, morals and manual arts.

The Meeting as an Educational Agency

THE MEETING served as an educational agency in four ways: first, it advised that children should attend the regular meetings for worship; second, it served as an agency of education on account of the fact that it either operated and maintained schools directly, or gave suggestions for the management of such schools; third, it published epistles dealing with the education of children; and fourth, it gave advice concerning books published for children, or undertook such publication itself.

In the first place, the meeting served as an educational agency in that it advised that children attend the regular meetings for worship. Children were expected to attend such services. As previously stated, these meetings were not child-centered; they were not planned for, nor participated in by children. In an indirect way, however, the children who attended meeting received training in worship and in religion in general. The Friends believed that religion was a gradual growth, and thus children would experience religion as they attended the meetings for worship and came to have their own experiences.

The place of children in the meetings for worship is clearly stated in the Epistle of 1723:

Then be concerned to keep them (children) to a constant, seasonable and orderly frequenting, as well as of week-day as of First-day meetings; instructing them to have their minds staid in the divine gift; to wait upon the Lord therein, to receive a portion with you of His spiritual favours.

This is typical of the advices issued frequently by the meeting. Children were expected to enter into the silent worship, wait upon God, and receive a portion of His Spirit.

In the early days of the Society of Friends, all the leaders were

of Life"; Allen Jay, "Autobiography"; Isaac Sharpless, "The Quaker Boy on the Farm and at School." All of these books deal with periods much later than the seventeenth century, but they are illustrative of the same principles as were developed in the earlier time. The first book makes a keen analysis of the place of children in the Friends' family.

young, many of them not twenty years of age. Their very youth probably made worthwhile and lasting impressions upon the children,
for these young preachers were heard by the children as well as by
the adults.

When George Fox started his search for the Truth, and began his
ministry, he was twenty years of age. George Whitehead was converted to the Quaker movement at the age of seventeen and began
preaching the following year. Edward Burrough was eighteen, and
Elizabeth Fletcher and James Parnell were sixteen when they became
"convinced of the Truth" and began preaching as members of the
Society of Friends. Elizabeth Hadden came to New Jersey as a missionary to the Indians when she was nineteen. William Hunt, who
was born in 1733, "when about fourteen years old, received a gift in
the ministry, in which he laboured with fervency and heart-awaken-
ing power."[56] George Newlan, who died in 1708, age nineteen, "in
his twelfth year was called to the ministry of the Gospel by the Giver
of all spiritual gifts."[57] Ellis Lewis, "about the thirteenth year of his
age (1703), appeared in public testimony of the Truth."[58] Robert
Barclay's daughter, Christiana, "in her fourteenth year, was engaged
to labour in calling others to repentance."[59] These statements indicate that young people and children had an important place in the
Society of Friends and that the meetings served as places of education
for the training in the ministry. Children were given opportunity to
take part in the activities of the Society at a very young age.

There are many records of "children keeping meetings," when
their parents were in prison. A reading Friend wrote to George Fox:[60]

Our little children kept the meetings up when we were all in prison, not-
withstanding the wicked justice, when he came and found them there, with
a staff that he had, with a spear in it, would pull them out of the meeting,
and punch them in the back, till some of them were black in the face.

Sewell says of the children at Bristol:[61]

It is very remarkable that children under sixteen years of age now performed what their parents were hindered from: these children kept up their
religious meetings as much as was in their power. But though they were

---

56. Philadelphia Tract Association, Biographical Sketches and Anecdotes of the
    Members of the Society of Friends, page 33.
57. Ibid., page 34.
58. Ibid., page 35.
59. Ibid., page 35.
60. Emmott, Elizabeth, A Short History of Quakerism, page 239.
61. Sewell, William, History of Society of Friends, Volume 2, page 275.

not within the reach of the law, yet once, nineteen of these youths were taken and carried to the house of correction where they were kept for some time. And though they were threatened with whipping if ever they returned to the meeting, yet continued valiant without fainting, although they suffered exceedingly from the wicked rabble. But so great was their zeal, that they despising all reproach and insolence, remained steadfast: and thus showed in spite of their enemies, that God would not suffer that the Quakers' meeting should be altogether suppressed, as it was intended.

Mrs. Emmott gives the information that in June, 1682, so many of the Friends of Bristol were in prison that the children of ten to twelve years of age, carried on the meetings. She wrote: [62]

The children kept up their meetings regularly, and with a remarkable gravity and composure.

It was surprising to see the manly courage and constancy with which some of the boys behaved on this occasion, keeping close to meetings in the absence of their parents, and undergoing many abuses with patience.

On the 16th, Tilly caused five of the boys to be set in the stocks, three quarters of an hour. On the 23rd, eight of the boys were put in the stocks for two hours and a half. On the 30th, about fifty-five (children) were at the meeting when Helliar with a twisted whalebone stick beat many of them unmercifully, striking them violent blows on their heads, necks, and faces, few of them escaping without some marks of his fury.

L. V. Hodgkin, in the book, "A Book of Quaker Saints," has a chapter on, "The Children of Reading Meeting." It is in story form and is based upon the facts as given by Sewell and Emmott. Some of the quotations from this book give interesting facts of children keeping meetings. The following quotation gives the dramatic story: [63]

Meeting? I thought thou saidst that all the Friends have been taken?

All the men and women, yes, but we children are left. We know what our fathers and mothers would have us do.

Yes, of course, we must show them that Friends are not cowards, and we will keep up our meetings, come what may.

Of course, children as well as grown-up people can wait upon God.

The children went to the meeting place, but found it locked. Finally, they met in a granary. The silence was broken by a half-whispered prayer:

Our dear, dear parents, help them to be brave and faithful, and make us all brave and faithful too.

The meeting was broken up and the children were whipped:

---

62. Emmott, Elizabeth B., A Short History of Quakerism, pages 249-250.
63. Hodgkin, L. V., Book of Quaker Saints, pages 293-298.

Still, Sunday after Sunday, through many long anxious months, God was worshipped in freedom and simplicity in the town by the silver Thames, Reading Meeting was held.

Thus it is shown that children were not only expected to attend meetings for worship, but in some cases they took part in carrying on the meetings when their parents could not do so.

The third way in which the meeting served as an educational agency was in the regular publication of epistles giving advices for the education of children. The epistles were the official statements of the yearly meeting. All advices, recommendations and warnings in regard to the education of the children are the best evidence of the attitude of the early Friends toward the education in religion, morals, secular subjects and manual arts.

It is of interest to note the wide variety of items which were included in the epistles. It indicates that the early Friends were greatly concerned with all the elements in the lives of children. The advices touch upon all four types of education, and they set the standards for the Friends' philosophy of education. They placed great responsibilities upon parents, meetings and schools.

The meeting assumed the authority of seeing that parents did not neglect their duty in the proper education of their children. If such a case was reported to the monthly meeting that body could send its representatives to those in care of children and urge them to be more careful in this matter.

There was something about a Quaker meeting which developed a spirit of reverence and which made education very real and powerful. Perhaps part of it was the general simplicity in the dress and manners of the worshippers, and in the meeting place itself.

There was never a question on first or fifth days whether or not the entire family would go to meeting. It might have been in the springtime of planting or the fall of harvest, or it could have been in summer heat or in winter isolation, but regardless of time, season or pressing duty—attendance at meeting came first. This training in regularity in attendance at religious gatherings helped the children to attain an exalted idea of religion. They realized that it was not something to "do" when convenient, but they learned that it was the supreme obligation and opportunity. Thus religion came to hold an important place in the lives of children. At first, they did not know why, and probably they did not dare to ask, but from their earliest days they were taught that meeting came first.

The method of meeting was the greatest educational feature. Children learned to worship in silence. Prayer became worthwhile and meaningful to them. They knew there was no set, "programmed" meeting of worship, and that there was no order of service to be followed. They might hear an elder say: "The Lord hath spoken," and they would wait to hear what the Lord had said. Passages of Scripture were quoted and explanations were given. Often a practical application of the lesson to the problems of life would be made, and the Friend might give some sound advice to the children and urge them to read the story from the Bible when they went home. The visiting minister from a far-off meeting, or perhaps from another country, would bring greetings and the children's horizon would broaden and the world would become larger. Many times the children were told of "our dear George Fox"; or of "poor little James Parnell who died in prison, for Truth's sake, at the age of nineteen"; or of Elizabeth Fletcher who became a minister when she was just sixteen years old and who suffered beatings and imprisonment for the Truth. Surely, someone would tell the children of the faithful children of the Reading Meeting, and urge them to be as worthy members of the Society. It would be certain that many would speak of the Inner Light, how it had guided them, and how the children should wait for its direction. And then someone would warn the children that they must look within themselves, and follow the guidance of the Light. And the children would be reminded that they must come to the experience of the second birth, by being "born again." Frequently concerned Friends would warn the Society, and particularly the children and young people, not to follow the "vain, corrupt fashions and customs of the world," and urge all to live according to the Truth. Such experiences were included in the religious education of children in the meeting.

The School as an Educational Agency

THE THIRD agency for the education of children was the school. The establishment of schools was the natural result of the Friends' interest in children, and their desire to bring them up "according to the Truth." The epistles and the advices, dealing with the education of children, could not have been realized without the organization of schools by the Society. A guarded education was impossible in the schools of private individuals or under the direction of denominations other than the Society of Friends. For these reasons, the early Friends developed a system of schools for the education of their children. Monthly and quarterly meetings were urged by the Yearly Meeting to organize and maintain schools. The various meetings were asked to contribute to their support. Children of poor Friends were also educated by the meetings.

The various meetings appointed special committees to have the general care of the schools. This committee appointed people to serve as teachers, helped outline the courses of study, arranged the financial matters, and had a general oversight of the schools.

It is impossible, in this study, to make a detailed or far-reaching investigation of schools among the early Friends. This has been done by other writers.[64] The purpose here is to recognize the fact, that from the first organization of the Society, schools were established; and to show that schools for all children played a large part in the theory and practice of the Society of Friends.

George Fox gave a great incentive for the establishment of schools. In 1668 he gave the advice which prompted the organization of the first schools for both boys and girls. He said:[65]

Then, returning towards London by Waltham, I advised the setting up of a school there for teaching children; and also a women's school to be opened at Shacklewell, for instructing young lassies and maidens in whatsoever things were civil and useful in the creation.

The statement "whatsoever things were civil and useful" became the central principle upon which schools were organized by Friends. It indicated the broad and practical nature of the system of education. It emphasized the vocational element, a theory which dominated Friends' educational theory and practice. It made it possible to organize education around the needs, abilities and opportunities of children. It is of interest to note that Fox gave such a general and

---

64. The Friends Educational Society was established in England in 1837. Records of the early schools are to be found in monthly, quarterly and yearly meeting minutes. For a study of the schools among Friends in America, for Colonial period see: Klain, Zora, Quaker Contributions to Education in North Carolina (Philadelphia, 1924); Woody, Thomas, Early Quaker Education in Pennsylvania (New York, 1920); Woody, Thomas, Quaker Education in the Colony and State of New Jersey (Philadelphia, 1923).

65. Fox, George, Journal, page 252.
George Fox frequently referred to the subject of education and was especially concerned with the religious and moral instruction of children, and the selection of Friends as teachers for Friends' children.

inclusive principle for the education of children, and that he included both boys and girls in his plans for schools.

In various places in his writings, George Fox discussed the problem of the different types of education for children. He was especially concerned that all schools should make proper provision for the religious education of children. He wrote to "all teachers and professors of Christianity," and asked them to examine the education of the children and see if it was consistent with the Bible. Fox objected to the following practices in the schools of his day, and the training of children in such things as: dancing, fencing, instruments of music, plays, shows, bear-baiting, bull-baitings, cock-fighting, nine-pins, cards, dice, football, wrestling, horse-racing and hunting for pleasure. He called them "vain exercises which spoil and corrupt the youth and ruin them in person and estate." He challenged the teachers to "shew Scripture for these things, seeing you profess it to be your rule."

Fox often had a deep concern for the type of teachers engaged in the education of children. He felt that the teaching profession was exceedingly important. He wrote to the teachers: [66]

I was much exercised, too, with school-masters and school-mistresses, warning them to teach children sobriety in the fear of the Lord, that they might not be nursed and trained up in lightness, vanity and wantonness.

One of the earliest advocates of education for children, particularly for the children of poor Friends, was John Bellers. In the following statement he showed the reasons for better teaching of poor children: [67]

And the poor have ill qualities and are as ill tutors, as well as evil examples to their children, and therefore it's of absolute necessity their children should have better instructors, and a more industrious education than their parents can give them; the happiness of the next age much depending upon the good education of this.

The nature of the guarded education, among the early Friends, and the general conception of their schools, is shown in a statement concerning the life and work of Evan Bevan who kept a school for Friends for thirty-five years. He was in accord with other Friends' writers as to subjects taught and freedom from the use of so-called "heathen authors." He placed religious education first, and was greatly concerned with the moral development of children. It is an

66. Fox, George, Autobiography, page 107.
67. Bellers, John, Essays about the Poor (1699), page 3.

interesting comment on both Evan Bevan and the system of education among the early Friends. It is said of Mr. Bevan: [68]

He instructed his pupils in the useful parts of literature, as Latin and Greek; and geography with various branches of mathematics; but he was chiefly concerned that they might be imbued with the love of virtue, and that by having religious impressions fixed on their tender minds, they might be preserved in innocence. He conscientiously declined instructing them in the heathen authors, lest they should acquire a disrelish for the principles of true Christianity. It was his general practice to assemble his family and scholars in the evening, for the purpose of waiting upon the Lord in silence thus initiating them in serious meditation and retiredness of mind; and as he felt his way opened, encouraged them in the performance of their moral and religious duties, particularly this of waiting in silence.

The character and task of the teachers was given careful consideration. First of all, teachers were to be members of the Society of Friends. They were to be worthy examples to the children. They were advised to give the children a careful, guarded education, keeping them away from the vain customs of the world. The teacher's task was not limited to any one form or type of education, but the task included all four types as outlined by the Society, and all were to be motivated by religion.

As the schools developed, teachers were urged to correspond with other Friends' teachers in order that they might become informed in regard to the best methods of instruction. It is of interest to note that this attempt at an association of teachers was primarily for the "children's advantage."

The moral training of children was emphasized and the teachers were advised to improve their students in this regard. The epistles suggested that Friends should: [69]

See that in all places, where schools are set up for the teaching of Friends' children, that the masters be diligent to improve and forward their scholars in learning, and keep them out of everything that would corrupt good manners.

Following the example and advice of George Fox in setting up the schools at Waltham and Shacklewell, Friends established many schools. Christopher Taylor had a Latin school for the Friends' children at Hertford. In 1674, a school for children of poor Friends was founded at Devenshire House in London. Another school was kept

---

68. Friends Library, Volume 13, pages 176-177.
69. Epistles, Volume I, page 89, Epistle of 1697.

at the Bull and Mouth Meeting House in London. In 1681, Richard Scoyer had a school at Southwark, and later at Wandsworth where he trained Friends to become teachers. In Bristol, a school was started in 1674. By the close of the seventeenth century the Friends had established schools in many places in England, Ireland and Scotland.

The earliest record of a Friends' school in Scotland is contained in the Edinburgh Quarterly Meeting for Twelfth month 1678:

> It being offered by Friends of Aberdeen that[70] they are about to set up a publick schooll for teaching Friends' children, by a Friend who is to teach reading and wryting and langwages and is likewayes to have inspection over their manners, the Friends generally is called for in the matter, and therefore it is laid upon the Friends here to acqwaint their respective monthly meetings.

In America the early Friends, following the practice and methods of English Friends, established local monthly meeting schools. In Pennsylvania and New Jersey schools were most numerous, although there were some organized and maintained in Maryland and Rhode Island. Friends were not numerous in other parts of New England and therefore, did not establish schools.

Some specific information in regard to Friends' schools in America, during this period before 1737, will show the theory and practice of early American Friends in regard to the education of children. In 1685, Thomas Budd[71] of Philadelphia, published an educational plan for the Colonies of Pennsylvania and New Jersey. The details of the system provided that children should attend school for at least seven years; that instruction should be given in religion, morals, arts and sciences; and that all children of both rich and poor, whites and Indians should be taught a trade. Mr. Budd believed that the schools should be supported by the government, but where this was impossible the schools were to be maintained by the local meetings.

The first educational adventure was at Newport in 1684. The Monthly Meeting gave permission to Christian Loddwick to "open a school in the Meeting House."

In Maryland in 1679, the Half Year's Meeting of Women Friends took up the subject of education and proposed the establishment of schools.

---

70. Journal of the Friends Historical Society, Volume VII, 1910, page 105.
71. Budd, Thomas, Good Order Established in Pennsylvania and New Jersey in America, pages 43 ff. My information was taken from Thomas Woody's two books referred to in my footnote 64, page 83.

Another illustration of early Quaker education is the William Penn Charter School of Philadelphia. This school was established in 1697 and was given charters in 1701, 1708 and 1711. The school was under the control of the "Monthly Meeting at Philadelphia." The poor were to be educated free of charge and the rich at reasonable prices. Fifteen overseers, "Discreet religious persons of ye people called Quakers," were in charge of the school.

In part, the charter of the William Penn[72] School contained the following:

Whereas, the prosperity and welfare of any people depends, in a great measure, upon the good Education of Youth and their early instruction in the principles of true religion and virtue, and qualifying them to Serve their country and themselves, by breeding them to reading, writing and learning of languages, useful arts and sciences, suitable to their sex, age and degree, which cannot be effected in any manner, so weel as bye erecting publict schools for the purposes . . .

Erect, support and maintaine a publict Schoole in the town of Philadelphia where poor children of both sexes may be taught and instructed in reading, writing, working and other good and useful literature, and maintained gratis, and the children and servants of the rich may be taught and instructed at reasonable rates.

The common seal of the school contained the words:

"Good instruction is better than riches."

Wherever the Society of Friends spread throughout Europe and America, schools were established and maintained. In these schools Friends developed high intellectual and spiritual qualities.

As public educational systems were developed, many of these schools were replaced by state supported institutions. However, the early attempts at the education of children stimulated later generations of Friends to provide academies, high schools and colleges for non-Friends as well as for Friends.

---

72. Penn, William, Charters of Ye Publick School, pages 6, 7, 11, 12, 24.

⊰ III ⊱

THE RELIGIOUS EXPERIENCES
OF CHILDREN

THE UNIVERSAL ignorance of child psychology until comparatively recent years is nowhere more apparent than in the records of the early Friends in regard to the place of children in their Society. During the period covered by this study, it was commonly assumed that children were small editions of adults, "little men and little women," with less experience and less learning to be sure, but with the same impulses, drives and capacities. It was understood that children were under the direction and control of the adults. While this was the situation among the Friends, it was also true of other groups in both America and England as well.

The early Friends were not different in most respects from the other folk of their time in their conception of the domestic, social and moral relations of children in the family and in society. There was no particular consideration of children from the viewpoint of their mental and emotional differences. In some respects the Friends' ideas of the religion of children were similar to those held by other religious groups, but in some ways they were entirely different. From the viewpoint of psychology of religion, Friends' views were similar to those held by the Puritans. Both Puritans and Quakers failed to recognize the significance of the mental capacities and nature of children; and they failed to understand the religious needs and interests of childhood. There was the general attitude that religion was religion, the Bible was the Bible, and that each should cause the same reactions in both adults and children. There were two other definite similarities, namely, the idea of "youthful piety," and the belief in immortality. The "otherworldly" conception held an important place in religion. This was evident to a large degree in Puritanism and the Quakerism of the period being studied.

As the Quaker children wore clothes cut in the same style as those of their parents, so the religion they were expected to make their own was an attenuated version of that which their parents confessed. It was assumed that they were able to share in the beliefs and practices of their elders. They were to make individual decisions to live according to the Truth, and this would involve a religious experience similar in many ways to adult conversion. It is true that the children could not leap at once to a complete appreciation of religion, but their growth in religious knowledge was the same in character as that of the adults. In writing to a child Isaac Penington gave a striking illustration of the point of view which regarded differences between children and adults as purely quantitative, and not qualitative. He wrote:[1]

And do not look for such great matters to begin with, but be content to be a child, and let the Father proportion out daily to thee what light, what power, what exercises, what straights, what fears, what troubles He sees fit for thee; and do thou bow before Him continually, in humility of heart, who hath the disposal of thee, whether to life or death forever. . . . But thou must join in with the beginnings of life, and be exercised with the day of small things, before thou meet with great things.

Some of the doctrinal talks the children heard must have seemed dull enough to them. The themes were taken from the circle of ideas which the Friends professed from the beginning and continue to profess to this day.[2] Among these are: faith in God, the Father, Creator and Preserver of all; faith in Jesus Christ the Son of God; faith in the Holy Spirit; faith in mankind as the children of God, with the consequence that all men are brothers; faith in the Inner Light which has power to lead all mankind to God; faith in the Scriptures which were given by the inspiration of God; and faith in the immediate communion between the individual and God. Children learned that all life is sacred and the sacraments are spiritual; that love is a creative and conquering power and should be applied as a method of living

---

1. Penington, Isaac, Works, Volume 6, page 509.
2. For an extensive study of the faith of Friends see the various editions of the disciplines of the different yearly meetings; and the works of the early leaders such as George Fox, Robert Barclay, William Penn, Isaac Penington, Edward Burrough, George Whitehead and others. For modern writers see Rufus M. Jones, A. Neave Brayshaw and others. Also see the various magazines of the Society. For complete titles see my bibliography.

by worthy members of society and that this was possible by the guidance of the Light Within; and that there was no need for an intercessor for each person might be his own priest.

There was nothing particularly new in this theology which was preached to young and old. Most of the beliefs were held by other independent churches of that time. Yet there were new combinations of faith, and new methods of expressing those ideals in daily living.

The greatest contribution of the Friends to religion was not in theology, but rather in the practical application of their faith. They insisted that religion was an active factor in everyday experiences. They believed that if religion was to be of any great value, it must function in the affairs of life. Religion was not a speculative philosophy, it was a practical ethic which grew out of a dynamic theology.

One of the particular ways in which the religion of the Friends came close to the lives of children as well as their parents was in the struggle for religious freedom. As previously pointed out the Society of Friends came as a protest against the formality and authority of the Church of England. In the seventeenth century England was in a political, social and religious upheaval and while Friends did not take a very active part in politics, they participated in a large measure in the social and religious movements. The subject of religious freedom was voiced by all the early leaders. They made a plea for "allowing liberty of conscience in the exercise of faith and worship."[3]

It was a long, hard struggle and for fifty years or more Friends were imprisoned and suffered untold persecution by religious and political enemies. Laws were passed against the Quakers and other religious groups, and five people could not meet together legally for the purpose of worship outside of the Established Church. With the restoration of Charles II, persecution increased for a time, but finally all were permitted to worship God according to the dictates of their conscience. By 1701 religious freedom had become a regular privilege and the Friends could say:[4]

> We have great cause to be humbly thankful to the God of all our mercies for that present ease and liberty we enjoy through the favour of the government.

3. Burrough, Edward, The Memorable Works of a Son of Thunder and Consolation, page 772. The same idea is expressed by Isaac Penington in his Works, Volume 2, page 175. It is a fact that all early leaders suffered greatly in the struggle for religious liberty. This is shown by a study of journals and memoirs.
4. Epistles, Volume I, page 100. Similar statements appear in the Epistles of 1707 and 1721.

The early Friends did not have paid, highly trained ministers to preach and pray for the congregation. There was no choir nor organ. There was neither incense nor procession. There was the simple, plain meeting house where Friends gathered to wait upon God and follow His directions. Silence did not mean that there would be nothing but silent waiting. The principles of obedience and freedom were to be practiced. The meeting could be entirely silent, or there could be speaking, singing or praying. What God directed, the worshippers must be free to practice. Barclay pointed out that: "our worship consisteth not in words, so neither in silence as silence, but in a holy dependence of the mind upon God."[5]

It was this worship based upon silence, obedience and freedom, which the children of Friends experienced from their earliest childhood. It was among the most direct and frequent religious experiences of children.

Children were warned not to rely upon the religious experiences of their parents. They were told that they would have to meet the problems of life and religion and make their own decisions and have their own experiences. If they could accept the faith of the Friends, then it could become their own faith. William Penn wrote to his children: [6]

Wherefore, dear children, let me interest you to shut your eyes at the temptations and allurements of this low and perishing world, and not suffer your affections to be captivated by those lusts and vanities, that your fathers, for the Truth's sake, long since turned their backs upon: but as you believe it to be the Truth, receive it into your hearts, that you may become the children of God.

This attitude of Penn explains the general belief of the Friends. They held that children could not inherit their religion. They might inherit a religious environment; they could be taught about religion; they could see examples of noble religious living; but if religion was to be real and to have a vital influence in their lives, children themselves must have their own religious experiences. Efforts of parents could not produce religion in the lives of children. Parents might give counsel and example, but the experience must be for each child himself.

The Friends tried to persuade children that religion was not something gloomy and sad, but rather pleasant and happy. Religion was

---

5. Barclay, Robert, Apology, page 336.
6. Penn, William, The Rise and Progress of the People Called Quakers, pages 78-79.

not merely for the silent, private times of life. On the contrary religion was to be practiced in all the daily events of the home, meeting and school life.

Children learned that while religion produced happiness, it often demanded intense suffering. They frequently heard the reports of the number of Friends in prison, the number who had died from suffering, and the plea for funds for the care of the needy. When a visiting Friend came to the meeting, he related the tragic stories of the sufferings of the Friends, and he told of the great faithfulness of all. Reasoning within themselves, the children came to know that religion was not something easy or meaningless, but rather that it was something which called for strength of conviction and courage of action. They saw that sacrificial service brought great joy and they learned that the true Christian was a happy person.

Descriptions of individual experiences of children are recorded in the writings of Friends. They are found in large numbers in the journals, lives, memoirs and personal writings of the leaders of the Society. They are also found in tracts, pamphlets, memorials and magazines published by the Society.

Children of the early Friends were quite normal in one respect, for their religious experiences did not always come easily, nor without conflict. One of the greatest causes for distress was the Quaker garb worn by the adults and children alike. Henry Hull (1730-1795) whose religious experiences had been developed by the time he was seven years of age when he heard a woman Friend "powerfully engaged in the ministry," said that he "dreaded to go to meeting or to school as there were few Friends in the city (New York) and my Quaker garb distinguished me as one, and the boys in the street would call me 'Quaker.' "[7] Such an experience would be a most disheartening one for a boy of seven, and one feels that the child had to pay rather dearly for his parents' "peculiarity" in regard to dress. Catharine Phillips (1726-1794) in her childhood[8] "experienced many conflicts" and her "convictions for evil were strong." Joseph Pike (1657-1729) before he was seven years old said[9] that "the spirit of the Lord began to work in my mind, and strove with me to bring me off from childish playfulness and vanities." Thomas Chalkley (1675-1741) records the following experience:[10]

7. Friends Library, Volume 4, page 236. Life of Henry Hull.
8. Ibid., Volume 11, page 188. Life of Catharine Phillips.
9. Ibid., Volume 2, page 357. Life of Joseph Pike.

I very well remember the work of God upon my soul when I was about ten years of age . . . I had been rebelling against God and my parents, in vanity and lightness . . . I heard a voice say unto me: 'what will become of thee this night, if I should take thy life from thee?' . . . Then I covenanted with God, that if He would be pleased to spare my life, I would be more sober . . . Nevertheless, I broke covenant with God my Maker, my adversary tempting me to do so, telling me I was but a child, and it was natural for children to brisk and play, and that God would wink at my childhood and youth and there was time enough for me when a man to be religious.

Closely related to the problem of conflict in religious experience were the elements of fear and sorrow. The earnestness of children is shown in such experiences. The absolute, unfaltering faith of children often came out of these fears and sorrows. These experiences are quite in keeping with the usual reactions of children. One need only to watch a group of children on a playground and see the seriousness with which they play their games or build their houses or stores. In much the same way they respond to religious stimuli, for religion is an important element in their lives and it calls for earnest attitudes and actions. A child is naturally "tender-hearted" and his sensitive spirit responds quickly and often sorrowfully. The fears and sorrows of children are illustrated by Stephen Crisp (1628-1692) when he wrote:[11]

When I was very young, about seven or eight years old . . . I learned to pray and to weep in secret, and to covenant with God for more watchfulness; . . . Yet this best state was accompanied with many doubtings and questionings, whether my evils were blotted out or not; especially when I saw I was again overtaken by the evil spirit, and led into evil thoughts, words and actions . . . Yet I knew that I wanted power to answer the requirings of that in me, which witnesseth against evil in me.

And when I was about nine or ten years old, I sought the power of God with great diligence and earnestness, with strong cries and tears; and if I had had the whole world, I would have given it to have known how to obtain power over my corruptions.

John Davies (1667-1744) was so effected by the experience of sorrow on account of his conduct that he said, "I often washed my couch with tears for my offenses against Him" (the Lord).[12] Joseph S. Elkinton tells of the distress caused by his religion, but shows the hope inspired in him by a kind and understanding father:[13]

---

10. Ibid., Volume 6, page 4. Life of Thomas Chalkley.
11. Tuke, Samuel, Memoir of Stephen Crisp, pages 28-29.
12. Friends Tract Association, Tract Number 74, page 2.
13. Elkinton, Joseph S., Selections from the Diary of, page 1.

I can well remember one evening when probably not over five or six years of age, having been brought to tears and under great concern because of a sense that all was not right between me and my heavenly Father, although no special sin was particularly before me, but there was a conviction that my heart was not good.

In his distress he talked to his father and his father gave him wise counsel and told him that he should "give place to such feelings," and he encouraged the boy "to hope in the mercy of Him who forgave those who repented and were concerned to mind the Good Spirit."

The Christian characters of parents and elders were the most potent influence in the religious experiences of the children. George Fox paid great tribute to both his father and mother and credited them with instilling into his young mind the qualities of true religion. It may be supposed that much of the interest and work of George Fox in the realm of religion resulted from his own experiences during childhood.

A tribute to the Christian family and a testimony of its lasting value, is given by Helen Cadbury Alexander when she says: [14]

In a home so full of beautiful Christian influences, it was very natural that Richard's (Cadbury) mind should turn with simple directness to the things of God, for as soon as he was old enough to understand anything, he had been told of the love of Jesus. His little heart was very tender, and one day when he was five years old, he ran to his small bedroom and kneeling down, asked the Lord to forgive him and be his own Savior. This incident might never have been known, but long years afterwards when one of his own children at the age of twelve, confessed Christ during a series of mission meetings Richard Cadbury had arranged for his work at Upper Highgate Street, he had a talk and prayer with her. It was then that he told of his own experience as a little lad of five.

Another religious experience of children was the sense of growth in grace. This is an interesting result for it is consistent with the working of the Inner Light. The leading from the Light came slowly and at first infrequently, but as the child came to rely upon its directions he felt a sense of gradual development in religion. It helped the child "to like very much to be better and more patient." [15] It led one girl to pray that she might "always walk in the narrow way and grow in grace." [16]

---

14. Alexander, Helen Cadbury, Richard Cadbury of Birmingham, pages 46-47.
15. Tract Association of Friends, Tract number 78, page. 2.
16. Forster, Joseph, Piety Promoted, page 255. Mary Hanbury (1797-1823).

One boy wrote in his diary: [17]

I am eight years old today. Oh God! I should like very much to be a better boy, and more patient and good than I am now. Be pleased to help me.

A year later he wrote:

I am nine years old today. I feel stronger than I did a year ago, for which I am thankful. I trust it will please Providence to make me a good boy; and willing to bear and suffer what He thinks right.

It was said of John Bateman (1732-1816) that he was sensible of divine grace when he was about seven years old and was "remarkably contrited in spirit at a meeting for worship held in silence." [18] Henry Tuke (1755-1814) was said to have been a lively boy, but when about thirteen "the forbearing principle of religion often gained the ascendency in his heart, and those opposing feelings were controlled and yielded to the gentle powerful influence of the spirit of Christ." [19]

John Woolman (1720-1772) tells of interesting childhood experiences in religion. He says: [20]

About the twelfth year of my age, my father being abroad, my mother reproved me for some misconduct, to which I made an undutiful reply; and next First-day, as I was with my father returning from meeting, he told me he understood I had behaved amiss to my mother, and advised me to be more careful in the future . . . Being thus awakened to a sense of my wickedness, I felt remorse in my mind, and getting home I retired and prayed to the Lord to forgive me; and I do not remember that I ever, after that, spoke unhandsomely to either of my parents, however foolish in some other things.

Some interesting records of children's experiences have to do with death and immortality. Like Christians of other groups, the Friends were greatly concerned with these two subjects, and the children shared in these interests. At times of sickness children instructed their parents, brothers, sisters and friends in ways of right living so that they would be "ready to die," and be assured of immortality. This is shown by the recorded experiences of children in their statements about death and immortality.

Children's statements about death reflect a decided adult influence, and they are stated in terms of adult experience. Some of the expres-

---

17. Tract 78, William Tyler Barling (1829-1839), page 2.
18. Evans, Thomas, Youthful Piety, page 126.
19. Ibid., page 79.
20. Woolman, John, Journal, page 21.

sions of children in regard to death and immortality are as follows: "offend the Lord," "willing to die," "my sins are forgiven," "I shall have a resting place in heaven," "resignation," "resigned to die," "may God's will be done," "need for forgiveness," "He died for us," "leave this troublesome world," "going to a better world," "the blood of thy dear Son," "He has preserved me," "may I be found worthy," "false pleasures of the world," and "freely given up to the will of God."

The story is told of a little girl who died at the age of six. She often talked to her parents about death and told them she would not live long. It was written of her: [21]

> The short, but exemplary and instructive life of this dear child furnishes abundant evidence that she had early submitted to the tendering visitations of divine grace, and carefully improved those outward means of religious instruction with which a kind Providence had blessed her. . . . After observing what grace accomplished in her, who was but an infant, surely none can say they are too young to become religious.

An eleven-year-old girl expressed a spiritual idea of immortality when she said: [22] "I shall die today and a grave shall be made and my body put in it, but my soul shall go into heavenly joy and everlasting peace." Another said: "the fear of death is taken away. I know I am going to heaven." [23] A boy who died at the age of thirteen said: [24] "I believe that the Lord is near to help me. I am going to a better world."

William Fennell, [25] who died at the age of twelve years, was often followed with the reproofs and convictions of God's holy Spirit. When he was sick he asked to have the Ten Commandments read to him. He was asked how far he had kept them and he said that he had not taken the Lord's name in vain, that he had loved his father and mother, and had not told lies or false stories.

Rebecca Toovey, [26] who died about the age of nine years, was a pious child. "Though she was but a young plant, it pleased the Lord to endue her with a large understanding in things both natural and divine."

---

21. Evans, Thomas, Youthful Piety, page 12, Elizabeth Secor (1814-1820).
22. Ibid., page 52. Mary Samm (died at twelve years of age).
23. Ibid., page 25. Jane Bennis (died 1840).
24. Ibid., pages 61-62. Jesse Cadbury (1805-1818).
25. Friends Library, Volume 13, page 130, Memoirs of the Life of David Hall.
26. Ibid., same reference as number 25.

It is of interest to see that the children thought that immortality was a spiritual condition of happiness. They believed that a future state of joy depended upon a present life of righteousness. There seemed to be no fear of death nor of a "burning hell." They believed that there was a better place than this world, and the duty of all was to live here so that the pleasures of a new condition with God would be the natural. result.

⤙IV⤚

BIRTHRIGHT MEMBERSHIP

THE GENERAL PROBLEM OF MEMBERSHIP

AFTER the Restoration of the Stuarts, with the return of Charles II, the acts enforcing worship in the Church of England were renewed, and persecution bore hard upon the Quakers. The Quaker Act of 1662 made it an offence to refuse to take an oath or to persuade others not to do so; and it made it illegal to assemble five or more persons under pretence of worship not authorized by law. The first and second offences brought fines and imprisonments, and a third offence could bring the penalty of banishment.[1] The First Conventicle Act of 1664, and the Second Conventicle Act of 1670, stiffened and extended the Quaker Act to all nonconformists.[2]

In defiance of the Acts, the Quakers met in large numbers, often by the hundreds. From the standpoint of both the church and the state, the Friends were outlaws. To refuse to pay tithes and to take oaths, to be found in a meeting of Friends, to preach the doctrine of the Friends, and to wear the Quaker garb were sufficient evidences that such persons were adherents of the Society. The Friends made no attempt to conceal their meetings. They frequently announced them in taverns, and held them in public places, often in the open. Altogether it was an easy matter to know that a person belonged to the Quakers. The children of Friends followed the faith and prac-

---

1. William C. Braithwaite in, "The Second Period of Quakerism," pages 22, 23, 112, 220, 226, 227 and 235 gives detailed illustrations of the application of the Quaker Act. Also see, A. Neave Brayshaw, "The Quakers, Their Story and Message," Chapter X.
2. On the application of these acts, see Braithwaite, above reference, pages 40 to 52, 64 to 81, 227, 265, 294, 356, 373 and 568. Also see George Fox, "Autobiography," pages 470, 474 and 475.

tice of their parents. They went with them to meetings and shared in their many sufferings.

There was no formal organization in the early days of the Society of Friends. The Friends were simply an informal group of people who believed, thought and acted alike. This informal character of the Society has raised the question whether there was any generally recognized distinction between members and non-members.

One of the most important and definite statements in regard to membership in the early days of the Society is given by William Sewel. He wrote: [3]

In 1648 several persons seeking the Lord were become fellow believers and entered into society with George Fox.

John Gouch in his "History of the People Called Quakers" (1789), frequently refers to "Members of the Society." [4]

The epistles are additional proof that Friends had membership from the beginning of the Society. In 1658 a general epistle was addressed to "Friends," and the duties of such were given. In 1659, the epistle urged: "that every member may act in his own freedom."[5] The fact that Friends were "separated" from the world, and "joined together in His blessed covenant,"[6] shows that the early Friends thought of themselves as members of the Society. The literature of Friends speaks of those who "profess with us."[7]

The Epistle of 1666 speaks of the "members of the church" and suggests methods of action "if any differences arise in the church, amongst them that profess to be members thereof." One of the tests of membership was the ability to stand by the faith of Friends in time of controversy, and if any failed to do so, they "ought to be rejected, as having erred from the Truth."[8]

In 1677, London Yearly Meeting issued an epistle in which it warned the Society against the separation among Friends in the North, where under the leadership of John Wilkinson and John Story, some of the Friends withdrew and organized separate meetings.

---

3. Sewel, William, History of the Christian People Called Quakers, Volume I, page 30. (Two volumes in one, New York, 1844. The first edition was printed in 1722).
4. Volume I, pages 166, 180, 250, 303.
5. Epistles, Volume I, page XXXIV.
6. Ibid., page XXXIV.
7. Ibid., page XXXIX.
8. Epistles, Volume I, page XL.

In 1681, the epistle advised the quarterly meetings to:[9]

Appoint one, two or more Friends to attend the assizes to make inquiry, what Friends are there presented or prosecuted for recusancy, or such like.

The same epistles asked Friends to send up to the Yearly Meeting their cases of suffering, to have Friends in London seek redress thereupon; to send up the names of Friends in prison, and the list of Friends who died in prison, with their names, age, dwelling place.

In 1710, the epistle voiced a particular concern for the "young convinced," and urged that they be early visited by "faithful Friends," that they might be given "encouragement, help and furtherance in the Truth." Happiness was expressed that the children had Christian experiences, and the meetings were urged to give special encouragement for them for their continued growth. It was shown that Friends believed that children had a definite place in the church, and they were encouraged to come to meetings, that they might have such religious experiences.

It is evident that, in the early days of the Society of Friends, there was an informal membership. This membership was not based upon belief in or recitation of a creed, nor upon an outward ceremony; but rather upon regular attendance at Friends' meetings, willingness to suffer imprisonment, confiscation of property, beatings and other persecutions for the sake of the "Truth." An important point, in this connection, is the fact that children, whose parents were members of the Society, belonged and that they shared fully, according to their abilities, in the thought and life of the Society of Friends.

While children were considered members of the Society, they did not assume the full duties of membership until they reached a proper age. The plan followed was to invite young men to "sit in" in the Men's Meetings for Discipline (business), and the young women to "sit in" in the Women's Meetings for Discipline. This was usually done when a young person reached the age of twenty or twenty-one, however there was no set age when a person automatically assumed responsibilities in the business of the Society. Admission to Meetings of Discipline depended upon the nature of the young people, and the choice and decisions of the elders. This is confirmed by A. C. Thomas when he says:[10]

---

9. Ibid., page 2.
10. From A History of Friends in America, A. C. Thomas. By permission of the John C. Winston Company, Publishers.

For fifty years or more after the founding of the Society, there was no regular membership; those who attended meetings and were believed to be converted and to hold views of the Society were deemed members. Such were invited to sit in the men's meeting, and also the children of such when old enough and thought suitable.

A definite illustration of how a young man was given admission to the men's meeting is found in the story of the life of Joseph Pike. Joseph Pike's father joined the Society of Friends in 1655. Joseph was born in 1657. He says that his parents, through the direction of the Truth, educated their children "in the nurture and fear of the Lord." When a young man showed by the nature of his life in keeping with the Truth, and when he proved faithful in attendance at meetings for worship, some member of the men's meeting would have a concern that such a young man should be invited to "sit in" the men's meeting. If the "sense of the meeting" seemed to indicate that all Friends were "in agreement" with this concern, the young man would be asked to attend. This was his permission to participate in the business matters of the Society. He did not need to join the meeting for, if one or both of his parents had been members at the time of his birth, he held a Birthright Membership. This step was a part of the natural process of growth in religious experience, and in the ability to share more fully in the thought and life of the Society. An invitation from the clerk or some appointed Friend, giving the desire of the men's meeting showed that the young man had met all entrance requirements.

THE ACTION OF 1737—BIRTHRIGHT MEMBERSHIP

As TIME went on, the followers of George Fox increased. Friends' practice of the care of the poor, and especially of poor children, and the educational opportunities for children influenced many people to associate themselves with the Society. Provision for children of imprisoned Friends called for a clear statement of membership. In the nation, religious toleration made progress. It was natural, therefore, that a more definite statement of membership became necessary.

In the year 1737, London Yearly Meeting approved a minute which defined membership in the Society of Friends. This minute gave formal approval and definite status to a membership procedure which had been practiced from the early days of the Society. The statement which gave legal status to membership is as follows: [11]

All Friends shall be deemed members of the Quarterly, Monthly, or Two-weeks Meeting, within the compass of which they inhabited or dwelt the first day of the Fourth Month 1737, and the wife and children to be deemed members of the Meeting to which the husband or father is a member; not only during his life, but after his decease, until they shall gain another settlement elsewhere.

For children, this method of membership was called Birthright Membership. A child, whose parents belonged to the Society, held membership from birth.[12] This minute approved in 1737 is one of the most important actions dealing with the place of children in the Society of Friends.

THE DISCIPLINES AND BIRTHRIGHT MEMBERSHIP

THE ACTION of London Yearly Meeting in 1737, in the formal adoption of Birthright Membership, was followed by other yearly meetings. As time went on and new editions of the Disciplines were published, articles were included in regard to the membership of children, and all editions accepted Birthright Membership.

The Rules of Discipline in regard to the membership of children, in New England Yearly Meeting, in 1774, stated:[13]

It is the sense and judgment of this meeting, that children of such parents as are married among Friends, shall be looked upon as members, and the children of such parents as become members by request, and are born afterwards, shall likewise be looked upon as members, as also their children born before, if their parents apply on their behalf, and the monthly meeting think they are suitable; and that where but one of the parents is a member, either father or mother, become so by application or otherwise their children shall not be looked upon as members, unless their father or mother professing with us make application to the monthly meeting on account of their children; and then the monthly meeting judge whether such children be suited to be admitted as members or not.

And it is advised that where but one of the parents is a member of our Society, that parents endeavour to bring up their children agreeable to Truth as far as it is in their power, and when they think it suitable for them to be members, not to neglect asking the care of Friends in their behalf.

---

11. London Yearly Meeting Minutes, Volume VIII, pages 314-319.
12. For further discussion of the origin of Birthright Membership, see: Brayshaw, A. Neave, The Quakers, Their Story and Message, page 181; Jones, Rufus M., The Later Periods of Quakerism, Volume II, page 108; Rowntree, John S., Quakerism, Past and Present, page 111; Thomas, A. C., and R. H., The History of Friends in America, pages 108-109.
13. Book of Discipline for New England (Providence, 1785), page 14.

London Yearly Meeting issued the following statement in regard to the membership of children, in 1820, and affirmed the same in 1833:[14]

On the subject of the right of children to membership in the Society, this Meeting considers it proper to define that such right is to be understood as extending to any child born of parents in membership, such parents having been married in a manner agreeable to, or not in violation of the rules of the Society; also, to any child, either the father or mother of whom is at the time of its birth a member, provided such father and mother were married agreeable to, or not in violence of the said rules.

In 1834, London Yearly Meeting made provision for the children who had not been entitled to Birthright Membership as follows:[15]

Children who have not a birthright in our religious society may be registered upon application made for that purpose.

The first Discipline of Iowa Yearly Meeting (1865), made the following statement in regard to the membership of children:[16]

All children born of parents, one or both of whom are members of our Society, shall be considered members.

The Baltimore Yearly Meeting of Friends, Hicksite, in 1902, issued a Discipline in which they added two features to the process of membership of children. The one was that the meeting applied to must be satisfied to receive the child into membership. The other point was that when the individual reaches the age of twenty-one, he must report, through the overseers of the meeting, whether or not he desires to remain a member. This last element is quite different from the usual Birthright Membership.

In 1917, London Yearly Meeting broadened its statement in regard to the membership of children to include those who had not been entitled to Birthright Membership. The rules of Discipline said:[17]

Monthly meetings are left at liberty, in their discretion, to admit into membership, in their infancy, any children whose parents are, or have been members, or children who are then otherwise connected with the Society, in cases where a reasonable probability appears that they will be educated in accordance with our religious principles.

---

14. London Discipline (1834), page 137.
15. London Discipline (1834), pages 227-228.
16. Iowa Discipline, page 38.
17. Christian Discipline of the Society of Friends (1917), Volume III, page 18.

At the same time, the Yearly Meeting issued a statement affirming Birthright Membership as the method of membership of children, and reminded parents to bring up their children in accordance with the principles of the Society.

The Philadelphia Discipline of 1926 gives an account of the membership of children, under the title, "Rights of Children." The statement is similar in most respects to other accounts of Birthright Membership. It does add the following note of interest: [18]

Children who are not members by birth may be received into membership by action of a monthly meeting in accordance with the procedure for convinced persons. If of suitable age, they may make application for themselves; in other cases application on their behalf should be made by parents or guardians.

In 1931, London Yearly Meeting issued a statement in regard to the membership of children. It contained the system of Birthright Membership, and gave an important place to birth notes. It also required the request of parents for the membership of children.

A study of the various disciplines of the different yearly meetings reveals the fact that rules in regard to the membership of children are practically the same. The 1931 statement of London Yearly Meeting is much more broad than the earlier statements. It is quite similar in content and method to Associate Membership, although it still recognizes Birthright Membership as the method of membership for children.

RECORDS OF BIRTH AND BIRTH NOTES

As EARLY as 1657, the Friends kept records of birth, marriage and death. The birth records contained the names of children; time of birth; names of parents; their residence; and a place for occasional notes.

From an early record of a meeting, probably held at John Crook's house in Bedforshire, it is found that birth records were kept, although no suggestion was made as to the use of such records.

It is not certain whether these records had anything to do with the membership of children, but probably they were used to prove a child's birth and to give him a certain status. Records were not kept

---

18. Faith and Practice of the Religious Society of Friends of Philadelphia and Vicinity (1926), pages 110-111.

by the government for nearly a century later, when the Registry Act of 1837 was passed.

A new and important significance was given to birth notes in 1848. After that date a birth note properly signed was necessary, to show that a child was entitled to Birthright Membership.

BIRTHRIGHT MEMBERSHIP, THE FAMILY AND CITIZENSHIP

UNDER the principle of Birthright Membership, the child has a definite status from his birth. He grows up as a member of the Society. He belongs. For a long time, the child does not entirely understand nor properly evaluate his birthright. If his membership is to become valuable, it must grow in worthwhileness.

The child's status, under Birthright Membership, is similar to his place as a member of the family. At first, as long as his cares are provided for, he is satisfied. But gradually he comes to realize that the family is a social, coöperative institution. He finds that there are certain family ambitions, ideals and responsibilities. He learns to appreciate his family inheritance. To be a member of the family, the child finds that he must make proper adjustments and find his place.

In a similar way, Birthright Membership may be likened to citizenship. A child of American parents is, at birth, an American. Immediately, he has a definite status. Although he cannot assume the full duties of citizenship until he reaches his majority, yet he does not wait until his twenty-first birthday to become a loyal, patriotic citizen. The child of American parentage has the opportunities and privileges of the Nation. Although he does not make the laws, he is represented in the law-making bodies, and he must obey the statutes. He has protection through American officers and courts. He may appreciate and use the beauties of nature. He may benefit by American, material opportunities. He has a great historical inheritance. The heroes of the nation belong to him. He may receive a schooling from the state from the kindergarten through the university. He has the privilege of entering into the economic, political and social life of America long before he votes. He is, in a large measure, and to his own knowledge, an American. From childhood, the boy has the feeling of belonging to the American Nation. It is his, and he is a part of it.

The child of Quaker parents is, at birth, a Friend. Immediately he has a definite status. Although the child cannot assume the full obligations of adult membership, yet he has some responsibility. He has opportunity to become a loyal, coöperative Friend. The child has free use of church property and buildings. He has a moral and religious protection and instruction. He has an extensive literary and doctrinal inheritance. The many characters of the Society, past and present, are his great heroes and examples. He is represented and provided for in the meetings for discipline. He is expected to attend the meetings for worship. He may be educated in Friends' schools from kindergarten through college. He may find many opportunities for service throughout his years of childhood.

While there are these many similarities between citizenship and Birthright Membership, there is one great difference. To take full responsibility of citizenship, the individual must reach the age of twenty-one, register and "be made a voter." Under Birthright Membership full standing is not prohibited until a given age. There are no definite acts to be performed. There is no time when the child's membership ceases, unless he withdraws of his own accord, or fails to follow the principles of the Society and is disowned. When the young person reaches a "suitable age" he is "invited to sit in" in the men's meeting for discipline, but that is a recognition of the assumption of a more complete responsibility, and not a different membership standing.

In the case of both the family and the nation, it is clearly understood that an habitual, thorough system of training is imperative. The child cannot become a coöperative member of the family, nor can he become a valuable citizen without much instruction and many widening experiences.

There are certain differences between the relation in the family and in the state. The child is always the child of his parents. He is always "flesh of their flesh, bone of their bone." Nothing can change this biological fact of nature. In the state, the child may adopt another nation than the one to which he belongs at birth. He may change his rights of citizenship by meeting the requirements of the other nation.

There are, also, certain differences between Birthright Membership and the family relation. The family connection is limited to a small number of people who share all the elements of life. Such a relationship is continuous. While members of a family may move into other parts, select other associations, and seemingly have little in common—yet the children always remain, at least physically, members of the family group. But, on the other hand, absence from meeting, association in other groups, particularly other religious groups, or the change of religious ideals are almost certain to lead to withdrawal from the meeting in which the person held membership at birth. If one is not active in a meeting, one soon loses place, if not membership.

BIRTHRIGHT MEMBERSHIP AS A GROWTH

NEITHER Birthright Membership nor citizenship are ends in themselves. They are means to ends. They are starting points for continuous growth in two of the most important elements of life. Both are fully appreciated and have most value with added interest and experience.

Children learn to value their citizenship after a long and varied program of education. Through the school, the home, the playground and patriotic events, citizenship becomes a great reality. The study of civics, government and history leads the children to knowledge of their country. Certain holidays, such as Independence Day, Armistice Day and Thanksgiving help the children to become true citizens.

In a like manner children come to appreciate their Birthright Membership. Through the home, the meeting and the school and certain events, such as quarterly meeting and yearly meeting, and special days such as Christmas and Easter, membership in the Society becomes a reality. The study of the beliefs, government and history leads the children to a true knowledge of the Society, and membership grows in meaning and value.

This growth process carries great assumptions and responsibilities for any group which practices Birthright Membership. It is the supreme problem in the place of children in the theory and practice of the Society of Friends. It is at this point that any system of membership or of religious education of children succeeds or fails.

To be more specific, the problem of growth is the problem of education. The method of entrance into the Society is of little importance. The supreme questions are: what kind of members do they become, and what means are used to help them to become worthy members of the Society? In other words, the dominant question is, what is the system of religious education?

These questions must be answered by parents, schools and meetings. Birthright Membership is a method of membership of children which places great educational responsibilities upon the Society of Friends.

The desire and hope of Friends have been that children would be brought up in a Friendly environment, acording to the teachings of Truth. It was expected that parents, schools and meetings would bring up their children in the fear of the Lord, and in a knowledge and appreciation of the doctrine and history of Friends. The great aim is to lead children to a personal acceptance of the principles and methods of the Society. The chief object is to educate children so that they would want to become, and would actually reach the state of "convinced" as well as Birthright Members.

But these great desires and hopes were not always realized as the following quotation suggests: [19]

It (Birthright Membership) is based upon the supposition that children born into Friends' families will be carefully reared in a knowledge of and love for our customs and testimonies. Unfortunately, this supposition is not always supported by facts. We have families of Friends willing but unable to train up their children to an intelligent understanding of their hereditary faith; and others who hold their birthright carelessly, making no effort to worthily discharge its obligations.

What Birthright Membership will mean to the child depends, largely, upon the teaching of both parents and meeting. Where it leads the children will depend upon their training in its theories, their opportunities for practice, and their responses in life situations.

Birthright Membership is an abstract and inanimate principle. In itself there is no particular power. It serves only as a status or starting point. The person holding Birthright Membership may live a life of cold indifference; or his membership may lead to an active, dynamic philosophy which functions in his world. Whichever course it takes depends upon proper stimuli. In order that Birthright Membership may be of real value, these stimuli must come from the home and the meeting. One writer suggested that Birthright Membership

---

19. Preface in the "First Day School Graded Course," Number 3, page 8, Tenth Month, 1916 (Philadelphia).

"is as the outer court; the inner court of the temple—the true church—
has yet to be entered into by a 'being born again.' "[20]

CRITICISM OF BIRTHRIGHT MEMBERSHIP

FOR over one hundred years there has been a strong controversy on
the subject of Birthright Membership. It has been entered into by
Friends in both America and England. It has been the cause of debate
for both Conservative and Progressive Friends. Friends' publications
have carried many arguments for and against this system of membership.

Many Friends have been in favor of Birthright Membership,
while others have opposed it. Some meetings still use it as a method
of membership for children, while other meetings have substituted
another method.

As early as 1815, John Moon wrote:[21]

I have long been dissatisfied with a rule amongst modern Quakers, which
brings their whole offspring into full membership in their infancy.

There arose the feeling that Birthright Membership was the chief
cause of decline in the membership of the Society. It was felt that
Birthright Members did not have a vital, energetic religion. It was
believed that many Friends were nominal members, and lacked any
true, personal religious experience.

C. H. Spurgeon, a non-Friend who was kindly disposed toward
the Friends, warned them in the following words:[22]

We love to see children of godly parents brought into church membership, but we would avoid above all things anything like hereditary profession or inherited religion; it must be personal in each individual, or it is
not worth a groat . . . I believe that the idea of Birthright Membership has
tended materially to weaken the strength of that most respectable and once
powerful denomination, the Society of Friends . . . Their children have
grown up to attend meeting, and to wear a particular garb, without receiving the spirit; certainly without that grand enthusiasm which honoured
their sires in days gone by.

In 1829, Daniel Wheeler, a member of the Society, wrote on the
decline of the Society of Friends. He gave as the reasons for the fall-

---

20. The British Friend, First Month, 1855, page 31, by "Z."
21. Moon, John, Observations and Quotations on Obtaining Membership, page 23.
22. The British Friend, Fifth month 2, 1864, article, "C. H. Spurgeon on Birthright Membership Among Friends."

ing off in membership: lack of persecution; worldly prosperity of Friends, accompanied with ease and indulgence; relaxation of attacks against the great enemy (Satan); and Birthright Membership.

Mr. Wheeler held that life in the Society of Friends was too easy. Children of Friends were born into a society which lacked the fervor and aggressiveness which had been so characteristic of the early Quakers.

It was also thought that membership in the Society of Friends was an inheritance, and that those not born in it had little or no opportunity to join its ranks. While this idea was largely theoretical, it did carry enough weight to be used as an argument against the practice.

CONFERENCES ON BIRTHRIGHT MEMBERSHIP

THERE arose such wide criticism of Birthright Membership that many conferences were held.

In 1889, New York Yearly Meeting appointed a committee to consider the matter of Birthright Membership. After some deliberation, the committee reported that they had considered the matter; that they were surprised to find so many Scriptural proofs for Birthright Membership (although they did not give such a list of passages); and they advocated the retention of Birthright Membership as the method of membership for children. The report of the committee was accepted and no change in regard to membership of children was made.

In 1900, the topic of Birthright Membership held a large place in London Yearly Meeting. There came a proposal to the yearly meeting: [23]

That children shall henceforth be enrolled as associates, with all the privileges now enjoyed by Birthright Members, except that they should not be members of Meetings for Discipline until they apply for full membership.

The plan was considered for two sessions of the yearly meeting. Some of the arguments used in the meetings were as follows:

One of the speakers said that only forty per cent of the Birthright Members remain even in "outward membership with us." He believed that Birthright Membership had led not only to a decline in

---

23. For a complete report of the Yearly Meeting discussion, see The Friend (London), Volume 40 (New series), 1900, pages 351 to 358.

membership, but a weakening of the fervor with which the principles of the Society had been held.

There was the general belief that people should be members of the Society, "not by flesh, but by their being born of the Spirit." This attitude seemed to have considerable influence upon the meeting, and upon the arguments against Birthright Membership.

The idea was expressed that children should, at some particular time be asked to say whether or not they wished to remain in the Society. It was believed that a decision time was most essential. In answer to this idea, one Friend gave testimony that there were many Friends of influence who, if they had been asked to decide definitely whether they would remain in the Society or not, would have left it.

One speaker on the subject urged the members of the Society to recognize the responsibilities toward its Birthright Members and help them to become Friends in "actions as well as in name." Another welcomed a discussion of the subject, but believed that a change of name would not "raise the spiritual tone of the Society of Friends." He made a plea for the Society to emphasize the many duties which went with Birthright Membership privileges.

For the conclusion of the discussion, the clerk formed and read the following minute:

> We would decline to make any alteration in our rules, but would impress upon the young the responsibilities of their Birthright Membership and the necessity for the spiritual membership also.

The minute met with the general approval of the yearly meeting and seemed to voice the sentiments of Friends. Thus, after a long discussion, London Yearly Meeting decided in favor of the practice of Birthright Membership, and uses it down to the present time.

The conferences of the Orthodox American Yearly Meetings, except Philadelphia, in 1897 and 1902 took action which greatly affected the standing of Birthright Membership in that body. There was no controversy on the matter, but the records show that Associate Membership was accepted in its place through the adoption of the Uniform Discipline which substituted that method of membership of children for Birthright Membership.

Another conference was held at Woodbury, New Jersey on Ninth Month, 9, 1921. About two hundred Friends, largely from the Eastern United States, attended. The conference consisted of papers on the subject of membership in the Society of Friends, and an open discussion by all who cared to take part. Arguments in favor of and in opposition to Birthright Membership were presented. At the conclusion of the conference, it was agreed that while Friends needed to be more faithful, yet they did not want to make change in the matter of Birthright Membership.

THE PRO AND CON OF BIRTHRIGHT MEMBERSHIP

A SUMMARY of the arguments for and against Birthright Membership reveals worthy viewpoints on both sides of the question. No topic, except the training of Friends' children according to the Truth, has held a more important place in the theory and practice of the Society. Provision for children has been uppermost in the minds of Friends.

The arguments which have been used to support the theory and practice of Birthright Membership may be stated as follows: that Birthright Membership gives the child a definite status in the Society immediately upon birth; that under Birthright Membership, religion is a part of the child's natural inheritance, since "children are an heritage of the Lord"; that Birthright Membership is consistent with the doctrines of the Society of Friends, especially the Inner Light, the original nature of the child, and the spiritual conception of the sacraments; that Birthright Membership is in accordance with the teaching of the Scriptures; that Birthright Membership makes possible the care of poor children, and the use of certain scholarships and funds; that this organic connection with the Society tends to keep young people as members, and gives them opportunity to grow in the faith and practice of the Society of Friends.

The Friends who opposed Birthright Membership gave certain definite objections to it and tried to show the bad effects which such a system had upon the individuals and upon the Society as a whole. Their side of the debate may be summarized as follows: that there was nothing gained by Birthright Membership which could not be had by other methods; that it made membership in the Society an inheritance, and prohibited free choice in such an important matter; that it failed to emphasize personal conviction, public confession, the need for conversion and the second birth; that it tended to lead to a nominal or technical membership, and in many cases to a mere social community rather than a religious fellowship; that there was not sufficient Scripture for the practice of Birthright Membership; that

Birthright Membership makes the Society self-contained as the members come from within and not from without the group; that it weakens the responsibility and emphasis for training of children for membership; and that Birthright Membership seems to weaken a program of religious education.

The foregoing arguments in favor of and in opposition to Birthright Membership were gleaned from periodicals and books. They cover a period of over one hundred years. The articles were written as separate and personal opinions, with little or no thought of using them as parts of a long and wide controversy on the subject.

Outside of the few conferences referred to, there was never an attempt to bring materials together to strengthen some side of a debate on Birthright Membership. As a person wrote, no doubt he gave his own personal ideas on the subject. He was writing for the sake of the cause. Writers seem to respond to criticisms evidently getting great delight in the matter. It was not uncommon to have a debate between two individuals take space in several issues of the periodicals. No doubt each writer fully expected some Friend of the same opinion or of contrary mind, to set forth in the following issue his own ideas on the subject.

The yearly meetings which have decided to keep Birthright Membership, as well as those which have decided to substitute another form of membership for children have passed judgment upon the arguments. But after all, the values and disadvantages of Birthright Membership—or any other form of membership—are determined by results. This matter is controlled by the individual and corporate membership. In the final analysis, however, Birthright Membership is judged by the lives of those people who hold such membership.

The study of the problem revealed that there are values and disadvantages in Birthright Membership. The facts that children have membership in the Society of Friends (in some yearly meetings) upon birth; and that their position in the Society may be a continuous growth have decided value. The fact that Birthright Membership gives regular standing in the Society of Friends is a great challenge and carries with it unusual responsibilities for the individual members, for parents and for the Society itself. Birthright Membership is rightly referred to as a preparation, "an outer court." It is not an end in itself nor a final or finished condition. To become members "in fact" and not merely "in name" is a practical and valuable challenge.

Birthright Membership, if it is to be of any great value, must lead into a life lived according to the Truth as held by the Society of Friends.

It is necessary to warn Birthright Members of this great challenge and opportunity. Parents and meetings must plan an adequate program of Quaker Religious Education in order that this system of membership may reach its highest and fullest values. The task must be shared by children, parents and meetings.

There are, also, several decided disadvantages to Birthright Membership, and those who argue against this system have a strong case. The history of the Society of Friends reveals the fact that formalism—the very thing the early Friends opposed so strongly—has been quite evident. The power and use of Birthright Membership is an illustration of this point. Silence which led to quietism is another. These have the same influence, in some sections of Quakerism, as rites or ceremonies have in other churches. Such a condition is a long way from the example of George Fox and other early Friends.

Closely related to this conception of Birthright Membership is the wrong interpretation of such membership as a part of one's inheritance. Arguments against this viewpoint carry considerable weight. If religion is to have value for children, or adults, it must be the result of a personal conviction which leads to public confession and a practical application of religious ideals. Such religion is not a mere verbal repetition of faith, but it is an expression of religion in all the problems and elements of life.

Whether Birthright Membership has good or bad effects upon individuals, parents or meetings cannot be determined with any degree of accuracy. Such an attempt would be a mere generalization. Individual differences greatly affect the religious development of persons, and a meeting is simply a group of individuals.

It would be unfair to Birthright Membership to hold it responsible for the religious growth or the religious indifference of individuals. It is but one of the many conditions or situations into which the child is born. It is a part of the child's social and religious background. While it should be considered in the evaluation of one's religion and one's character, it is but one factor bringing either good or evil effects.

An argument of very great importance is the assumption that nothing is gained by Birthright Membership which could not be had by some other form of membership for children, and in the substituted method most of the objections, if not all, could be eliminated. Here again, comes the matter of measuring religion. It is probably safe to say that it would be impossible for all yearly meetings of Friends to reach an agreement on a definite statement of the true faith and practice of the Society. Therefore, it would be impossible to determine whether Birthright members are better or worse than other members.

The problem of testing the values and disadvantages of Birthright Membership is not for one isolated, fact-desiring individual. It is too personal to be reduced to a survey or questionnaire. It is, rather, for the Birthright member and for the meetings which practice that system of membership to make the test. From the standpiont of the Society of Friends the testing program should be a definite part of the methods of religious education. Such a task relates particularly to a study by the local and yearly meetings.

The values of Birthright Membership are subjective and not objective. They are within the individual and must, to the greatest degree of accuracy, be measured by the person himself. The life contribution of any member is the final test and the ultimate value of a system of membership.

The practice of Birthright Membership is valuable because it gives children the feeling of belonging to the Society of Friends from infancy. This is of considerable worth because religion becomes a definite part of the regular joys and obligations of life. Children do not have to feel that religion is something for adults, alone, but from their own experiences they know that they may share in the great advantages of the meeting. The adults, as they look back upon life, know that they grew up in the church, and that religion has been a practical, motivating power in their lives.

Again, Birthright Membership is valuable because it is consistent with the doctrines of the Society of Friends. Since the Quakers reject infant baptism, original sin and predestination; and advocate the doctrine of the Inner Light it is logical that children should be given membership in the Society immediately upon birth. The belief that religion is a continuous growth, and that it comes largely through the leading of the Inner Light makes Birthright Membership a good starting point for religious development.

The weakest point in the theory of Birthright Membership is the fact that it minimizes the necessity for conversion and the second birth. On the other hand, however, this point could be a strong argument in favor of the Inner Light—the guidance and revelation directly from God, and the great need of religious education. Because Friends believe that the second birth is essential, they can think in terms of a gradual growth in religious experience, and not in a sudden turning away from sin. At this point the Friends' principles of education, in particular the idea of a guarded education, are of great value. Birthright Membership is consistent with the Friends' views of doctrine as pertaining to children, and it necessitates a thorough system of *continuous religious education.*

The proposition that Birthright Membership is consistent with the teachings of the Scripture is valid. While the Bible does not advocate any definite system of membership for children, it is true that Jesus gave an important place to children and pointed out that men must become as little children if they are to enter the kingdom of heaven. The innocency of children is a common teaching of the Bible. However, most of the biblical passages used for or against Birthright Membership seem rather beside the point and do not add much value to the arguments.

The objections to Birthright Membership appeared more frequently and seem more logical and in accordance with psychological principles than do the arguments in favor of it. Birthright Membership came to hold such an important place that it took on the aspects of a rite. Friends put great reliance upon Birthright Membership, they considered it as an inheritance and it carried the usual faults of any inheritance.

The argument that Birthright Membership would keep young people in a church simply because they were born into it, although they might never reach the point of decision in favor of Friends' principles, is a weak proposition. Such members would not experience true religion, nor would they be of much value to the work of the Society. If adults advocate Birthright Membership because it keeps the young people in the Society, it shows that such people have based their religion upon fear and not upon faith and personal experience.

To advocate Birthright Membership because it makes possible certain funds is a weak argument. Benevolent people of the right character and purpose could be found who would willingly give funds for the education of all needy children regardless of the method of membership. Wise counsel on the part of ministers and school administrators could eliminate any difficulties in this regard.

The argument that Birthright Membership tended to do away with the belief that the second birth was necessary is one of the strongest propositions. It can be seen that the self-complacency which came with an inherited membership, and with the reliance upon the Inner Light to the exclusion of education, would do away with the feeling of need for conversion and rebirth. This indicates that children would not be led to a personal experience and religion would not hold a place of any great significance. The chief value of the idea of the second birth is the fact that the individual does not have to turn away from a life of sin necessarily, but rather that he comes to a place of personal decision for and an acceptance of the ideals and teachings of Jesus. Thus, the child upon reaching the age of accountability would have to decide, for himself, the way he desires to live. Without the experience of personal acceptance, religion would tend to become purely nominal.

An evaluation of Birthright Membership cannot ignore a study of individual persons. The system of Birthright Membership is weak or strong as those who hold it come to be weak or strong members of the Society. Systems and organizations are inanimate and follow the directions of people. They fail or succeed in proportion to the failure or success of their followers. This is true of Birthright Membership.

$\prec V \succ$

ASSOCIATE MEMBERSHIP

THE controversy on Birthright Membership brought the whole subject of the membership of children before the entire Society of Friends in a most free and frank manner. Both the advantages and the disadvantages of the system were clearly shown, and ample opportunities were given for the improvement or the complete rejection of the system. In the democratic organization of the Society there was no officer or council which could force any method of membership upon Friends. Each yearly meeting was free to retain Birthright Membership or adopt some other form of membership for children. This resulted in the continuation of Birthright Membership by some yearly meetings and the rejection of it by others.

SUGGESTED SUBSTITUTES FOR BIRTHRIGHT MEMBERSHIP

THROUGHOUT a period of years a number of suggestions were offered as substitutes for Birthright Membership. These were as follows:

Preliminary Membership

AMONG the first suggestions for a substitute for the system of Birthright Membership was one by Robert Barclay in 1872. He recommended a preliminary or trial membership.[1] This was to be offered to all people who were not able to accept active membership. People were to be accepted in this capacity "if willing of their own accord to come under religious instruction and oversight." Such people were to attend Bible, Christian principles and Friends' doctrine classes in preparation for full membership.

---

1. Barclay, Robert, On Membership in Society of Friends, pages 60-61.

Finally, these preliminary members who reached a "state of confession of faith," and had a desire for active membership were to be admitted. Barclay believed that such an arrangement would do away with the evils of Birthright Membership and that it would greatly enlarge and vitalize the Society of Friends.

This suggestion carried many values. It gave a definite status to the child, and it led to faith and confession. This naturally led to personal decision and commitment. It implied a thorough system of religious education.

The chief objection by Friends was the fact that the method called for a confession. Friends had always objected to a confessional. They raised the questions: of what should the confession consist; when should the confession be made; to whom should it be made; and who was to judge whether the candidate passed the requirements of the confession? So serious were these objections that such a system could not have any great support by the Society of Friends.

Probationary Membership

A SECOND suggestion for substitution was given by William Lloyd, in 1885. He favored doing away with the membership of children and thought they should be considered as "under the care of the Society," until they reached a "suitable age" when they should be "pleasantly queried" by the Society. This was referred to as a probationary membership. The idea in detail was:[2]

All children born of members or one parent a member to be enrolled as under the care of our Society and entitled to all of its privileges.

Give all Friendly young people the privilege of attending our business meetings and receiving the Society's varied instructions.

Make the business of the meeting (with the aid of the parents) to impart unto these, according to their years, a simple yet intelligent teaching of the practice and principles of Friends.

At suitable age have them pleasantly queried with as to whether they expect to remain with Friends or go with some other denomination.

Give five years of probation to finally decide their membership, still furnishing to these continuous instruction from lip and book, with frequent opportunities of asking of Friends a reason for the faith that is in them.

Let it be the duty of intelligent Friends to occasionally invite persons not attached to any Society to come to our meetings and see if they cannot aid in making them more helpful to the community.

2. The Friends Intelligencer, Volume 42, 1885, page 296, article by William Lloyd.

This suggestion had many of the values of the former idea. It called for a definite time of decision for full membership and this would eliminate one of the greatest difficulties with Birthright Membership. It had the added value in that it opened the Society to visitors. It emphasized a thorough and continuous religious education.

There were certain criticisms made. First it was very poorly named. Many objected to the name probationary, as it sounded too much like the court term dealing with offenders. Some thought that the statement "suitable age" would bring difficulties. It would be a problem to determine when an individual had reached such an age. This method never found many advocates.

Decision at Twenty-one Years of Age

A THIRD suggestion, quite different from the other two, was the idea of Birthright members reaching a decision when they attained the age of twenty-one, whether or not they would remain in the Society. The theory is stated as follows:[3]

I would suggest that at the age of twenty-one years, their Birthright Membership should cease, and they should make request to be admitted on their own responsibility, and if they are in unity with our principles, they should be received into the Society as convinced members.

This idea had two good elements: it would keep the children in the Society and would give them a definite membership standing at least until they were twenty-one; and it would make personal decision and application for membership an essential. Furthermore it would give the Society an opportunity to grow into a group of truly convinced Friends.

Children of Members

IN 1899 a fourth suggestion was made which was similar to the probationary method. It presented the idea that children should be known as "Children of Members." The meaning of the idea is given as follows:[4]

Until children become of age and desire active membership, they should not have a membership, but should be known as children of members.

---

3. The Friend (London), 4th Month 17, 1896, page 252, in an article by Mangnall, Abel.
4. The Friend (London), 11th Month 3, 1899, page 717. In an article by W. H. F. Alexander.

Thus, gradually, the time will come for the adolescent member to apply for full rights of membership. Recognizing the extreme diversity nature shows us in physical, mental and spiritual development, we should fix no time limits. Our young people should begin as attenders. This ought to give the Society 'convinced Friends' less hampered than today by paper-members and other dead weights.

This method, as the others, would correct some of the dangers and difficulties of Birthright Membership, and it offered a valuable substitute. Its chief values are the recognition of individual differences in the physical, mental and spiritual nature of people; and the necessity of personal decision and application for membership in the Society.

At the same time, one Friend seemed to favor doing away with membership for children, and suggested that they wait until they reach an age of ability to decide for themselves. His idea was hardly a suggestion for a substitute for Birthright Membership, but it is given to show the general attitude toward the subject: [5]

It is plainly wrong to admit to church fellowship any but those who through repentance toward God and faith toward our Lord Jesus Christ, have experienced the all-important change known as conversion or the new birth. Joining the church ought to be profession of faith in Christ and of dedication to His service.

True to the conviction of Friends, this idea assumes the need for complete dedication of the individual to the cause and doctrine of the Society, with special emphasis upon the place of Jesus Christ. It also recognizes the need of conversion, and it includes the idea of service. This suggestion shows the extent to which the desire for improvement of membership had gone.

Junior Membership

ONE of the most reasonable suggestions came from a committee of Friends from Shaftesbury, Bristol and Wincanton, England. This method was called junior membership. The theory was stated as follows: [6]

Junior membership should date from birth of all children either or both of whose parents are in membership at the time of the child's birth, with notification of birth.

5. The Friend (London), 11th Month 17, 1899, page 760, article by Alfred Robson.
6. The Friend (London), 4th Month 23, 1920, page 248.

Junior membership to carry similar privileges in regard to education, attendance at business meetings, but to cease at the age of twenty-five if no decision has then been come to.

Junior members are to be encouraged to consider full membership.

The Society is to exercise the same care and solicitude toward junior members as hitherto has been the case with regard to Birthright Membership.

The proposed junior membership met with considerable disapproval, particularly because there was fear that the young people, at the age of twenty-five, would not ask for membership. Some Friends held that such a system of membership would force the Society to accept a statement of belief or creed, and that the Society of Friends would become like other denominations "with outward observances." These objections undoubtedly carried great weight in London Yearly Meeting, and kept the Society from accepting this suggested substitute for Birthright Membership.

Eight months later a similar idea was given by Joseph Smithson when he proposed "a junior membership that was the gift of the church; and an adult membership that was the choice of the individual." [7]

As with the other suggestions, this method required that a decision time was necessary, and that religion in the Society should lead to an active, powerful membership, and that it must be the choice of the individual.

The Revised List of Members

A SUGGESTION quite different from all the others came from Joan Mary Fry. She proposed that: [8]

Every meeting keep a list of those who attended a certain number of times during the year, and also the children of such. At the beginning of each year let the overseers revise the list and, at the end of three years, simply omit the names of those who have not met the required number of attendances during the three years.

In The Friend (London) of fourth month 8th, 1921, Douglas J. Manning objected to such a system of membership. He disliked the idea of "ticking off" people as they came to meeting. He felt, also, that some people would simply attend the required number of times,

---

7. The Friend (London), First Month 1921, page 28.
8. The Friend (London), Third Month 25, 1921, page 186.

but would not show any more interest in the Society than under the method of Birthright Membership. He referred to a former suggestion that all overseers should feel the responsibility of approaching the Birthright Members when they reached maturity (purposely unspecified) and inquire if they desired to retain their membership in the Society.

A General Ratification of Members

ANOTHER suggestion was to retain the present form of membership but add to it "a general ratification of membership, say every five years. All members over twenty-one (or twenty-five) years of age should be called upon to ratify."

Neither the ticking off process nor the general ratification ideas appeared more than once, nor did they lead to any action by the Society of Friends. These methods were too general and did not meet the problems involved in the membership of children.

The history of the membership of children in the Society of Friends shows that these suggestions offered as substitutes for Birthright Membership ended as suggestions. Neither the preliminary membership, probationary membership, decision at twenty-one years of age, children of members, junior members, revised lists, or general ratification ideas made sufficient impression to be accepted by Friends.

ASSOCIATE MEMBERSHIP

EVENTUALLY The Five Years Meeting of Friends in America rejected Birthright Membership and substituted Associated Membership as the system for children.

The Third Quinquennial Conference of Orthodox American Friends, except Philadelphia Yearly Meeting, met at Indianapolis on Tenth month 19, 1897. Two very important decisions were reached: first, that the Society of Friends should work toward a closer union of American Yearly Meetings; and second, that there should be a Uniform Discipline for the yearly meetings which should join in the proposed union.

Prior to this time there was little unity or coöperation. While each yearly meeting had recognized London Yearly Meeting as the example in organization, discipline and doctrines, there was no official or binding connection between the American Yearly Meetings and that body. Each yearly meeting had carried on its own affairs and had followed its own discipline.

At the above mentioned conference, a committee was appointed to formulate a Uniform Discipline and report to the conference to be held Tenth month 21, 1902. Between the years of 1897 and 1902, the committee worked out the plan for a new, Uniform Discipline. As the work progressed, statements in regard to the matter were printed from time to time in The American Friend. Finally, the entire proposed discipline appeared in that paper in the issue of the Twelfth month 14, 1899. In this way opportunity was given for all Friends in the various yearly meetings to become familiar with the proposed discipline and consider it in local meetings or through the press. It is most surprising to note that there was very little comment or discussion on the subject of change of membership of children. Only two articles appeared in the American Friend which seemed to be closely related to this problem. One article[9] on "The Place of Children in the Church" advocated Associate Membership because it gave a place to the children and placed the responsibility of choice of membership upon the young people themselves when they reached the age of accountability.

One other statement which appeared in The American Friend helped answer many questions, and clarify the meaning and purpose of Associate Membership. The statement is:[10]

The question has been raised whether, under the Uniform Discipline, the children already enrolled as Birthright Members are to be counted as active or as Associate Members. There has been but one view in the minds of those who have framed the Discipline, which is that the children who were born before the Discipline was adopted are active members. . . . A Friend's child has a vested right of membership under the old system. Those, however, who are born hereafter, in yearly meetings which have adopted the Uniform Discipline will be enrolled as Associate Members.

Another question may be asked: When shall Associate Members be received into full, active membership? There can be but one answer—just as soon as they are ready for it. It is not something to be settled by a definite age limit. Some children of ten are much nearer the kingdom and much more fitted for membership in the church, than are other persons at forty. There should be no unnecessary delay in receiving all who show that they are conscious of life for and faith in Jesus Christ. The more important

9. Article by Mary Kimber, 7th Month 4, 1901, page 634.
10. Editorial, The Child in the Church, 2nd Month 6, 1902, page 124. (Rufus M. Jones was editor at the time.)

question, however, is how shall the church fulfil its responsible duties towards children, and how shall it prepare them for membership? We spend a hundred times more effort in discussing some speculative doctrine which is no nearer settlement now than in St. Augustine's day, than we do on the practical question of how to bring these lambs to the Master and how to train them in the truths of the Gospel.

The proposed discipline was presented to the various monthly and yearly meetings. It was adopted by the Yearly Meetings of New England, Wilmington, Indiana, and Kansas in 1900; by California, New York, Western and Baltimore in 1901; and by Oregon, North Carolina and Iowa in 1902.

In 1902 the Fourth Quinquennial Conference was held. Two actions of great historical importance were taken. The one was the formation of the Five Years Meeting of Friends in America; and the other was the adoption of the Uniform Discipline. The Yearly Meetings which composed the Five Years Meeting, upon its organization were: Baltimore, California, Indiana, Iowa, Kansas, New England, New York, North Carolina, Oregon, Western and Wilmington. Canada Yearly Meeting joined in 1907, and Nebraska in 1908. Oregon Yearly Meeting withdrew in 1926. Kansas withdrew in 1934.

The most important and radical change in the Uniform Discipline was the substitution of Associate Membership for the traditional Birthright Membership. In 1902, the body of Friends having the largest membership, greatest spread in territory, and most organized coöperation rejected Birthright Membership and adopted Associate Membership.

The Uniform Discipline sets forth the meaning and nature of this form of membership in a clear and definite statement. It defines the procedure to be followed in the application and acceptance of children as members of meetings which belong to the Five Years Meeting. It is a very complete statement and defines the character and responsibilities of one who seeks admission into the active membership of the Society of Friends.

The statement adopted by the Five Years Meeting defines Associate Membership as follows: [11]

The Friends admit into membership all who make a profession of faith in the Lord Jesus Christ, whose lives testify to their union with Him, and

---

11. Constitution and Discipline for the American Yearly Meetings (Adopted by New York Yearly Meeting of the Religious Society of Friends—1901), pages 17-18.

who accept the doctrines of the Gospel as held by the Friends. The children of members are enrolled as Associate Members. They are thus recognized, not because their birthright can of itself make them members of the body of Christ, for they can only become such by experiencing the new birth by the Holy Spirit, but because of the promises in the Holy Scriptures to believers and their households, and the conviction that true Christians will so make their children the objects of living prayer, and will so instruct them in the Gospel and go with them to the Throne of Grace, that they will surrender their hearts to God in their youth, and early take a natural and living interest in the Church as they do in the family. Persons thus enrolled as Associate Members shall be enrolled as Active Members of the Church when they shall have made a credible profession of faith in Jesus Christ as their Saviour and Lord, and shall have accepted the doctrines of the Gospel as held by the Friends. If the member does not make such profession when he reaches matured years, his name may be dropped from the list of members, at the discretion of the monthly meeting. Where but one parent is a member the children may be enrolled as Associate Members upon the request of that parent and with the consent of the other.

Thus, Associate Membership came into existence as the method of membership of children, in those meetings belonging to the Five Years Meeting of Friends. From 1902 down to the present time that method has been practiced by those Yearly Meetings.

The distinct features of Associate Membership are found in an analysis of the statements in the Discipline. They have a direct contribution to make on the place of children in the theory and practice of the Five Years Meeting of Friends.

In the first place, under Associate Membership, full membership standing is not a gift nor does it come with birth. It comes at maturity when the young person has reached the age of accountability, or during adult years. The person himself decides when he will apply for membership. Associate Membership gives the child a definite status, but not a continuous one. He is an associate, in a sense a junior member. Both the child and the Society of Friends are on trial. Both have definite responsibilities and opportunities.

Before the child can become an active member, two things must happen. First, he must reach the age of decision so that he may choose for himself; and he must show a true belief and active interest in the Society. Secondly, the Society must give adequate instruction, ample opportunities for self-expression, and agreeable associations so that the child will want to be a member in full standing.

The Associate member has all the advantages and privileges of the Society. The program of the church is graded according to the abilities and needs of children. The child is given moral and religious instruction and example. Whether his parents belong to the Society or not, makes no difference. All children receive the same instruction and opportunities.

The Associate member is a part of the meeting. He hears and reads about the ideals and heroes of the Society. He may accept them as influences in his own idealism and conduct. Quakerism may become a guiding factor in the daily experiences of life. The child is invited and welcomed to the meetings of worship and business. He is desired and sought as a student in the schools and colleges of the Society. He is given many chances for service in and for the Society of Friends.

An Associate member is never disowned. If he withdraws, at any time, there is no stigma of disgrace. He has not broken a continuous standing in the church. There is no feeling of cast or clique, on account of his birth or inheritance. At all times he is free—free to remain in or withdraw from the Society. He is free to act according to his convictions.

Associate Membership leads into one of two different directions. It may lead to withdrawal from the Society, or to an active membership within it. The action is determined by each individual person. If he makes a profession of Jesus Christ and accepts the faith of the Friends, he may become an active member. If he feels that he is out of agreement with the Society, or for any reason does not want to become an active member, the matter is regretted by the meeting, but the individual's name is removed from the list of members and the individual is free to associate himself with some other religious group. If the associate member continually absents himself from meeting and shows no interest in the Society, "at the discretion of the monthly meeting" his name is taken from the list. If the member decides to withdraw, there is no feeling that he has sold his birthright. He has simply chosen one of the ways made possible by Associate Membership.

Associate Membership is consistent with the Quaker belief in the personal, inward experience of religion. At the age of maturity, the person must decide whether he will remain in the Society and become an active member or whether he will withdraw. If he remains he must have a personal conviction. He must have the experience of the second birth.

This form of membership serves as a stimulus to constant endeavor. It stimulates the child, the parents and the meeting. Associate Membership does not carry with it the feeling that the child belongs to the meeting, that he is already one of God's select people, and that nothing more needs to be done. The fact that a decision must be reached sometime, and that membership in the Society of Friends is a matter of faith and practice, leads the individual to thoughtfulness and activity. Membership is the result of steady, purposeful growth. Thus the person senses the meaning, responsibility and value of membership in the church. Parents and meeting will attempt to develop methods which will lead the Associate member to a personal acceptance of Quakerism and an active participation in the work of the Society. Both parents and meeting will be anxious for the child to assume the responsibilities and to enjoy the privileges of active membership and they will be greatly concerned with the religious education of the child.

Associate Membership tends to lead to an active membership rather than to a nominal one. But, where Associate Membership leads depends upon the individual holding such a membership, and the meeting to which he belongs. This system of membership, as well as other systems, is successful in proportion to the success of the religious educational program of the meeting. Personality again becomes the element of greatest importance.

The strongest points in favor of Associate Membership are: that it is a preliminary and not a continuous status; that it gives the child a definite membership standing; that it offers the child full privileges, according to his abilities, desires and interests; it must lead to a personal conviction and a public confession, or it ceases to be; it is consistent with Friends' doctrines; it tends to lead to a vital, active membership, rather than to a nominal one; it requires a thorough program of religious education; and it serves as a proper stimulus for children, parents and meetings.

Before the next Five Years Meeting, criticism of the system of Associate Membership had begun. In 1906, Plainfield (Indiana) Quarterly Meeting discussed the matter and requested the Yearly Meeting to ask the Five Years Meeting to eliminate Associate Membership. The request came to the Five Years Meeting of 1907, and in keeping with the usual democratic procedure the matter was given careful consideration.

The details of the petition are:[12]

First, Associate Membership is unscriptural, for the reason that all children are provided for in the atonement of Jesus Christ and are saved members of the invisible church until they have sinned by actual transgressions. The promise of Christ extended to believers and their households.

Second, Associate Membership provides for a relationship to the church which will be lightly esteemed by persons holding it, inasmuch as it confers no obligations or responsibilities, and has practically no binding force to the church.

Third, Associate Membership opens a wider door for leakage in membership than any system the church has ever adopted.

Fourth, Associate Membership has already and will continue to lead to a very serious complication of our record books, since two separate lists must be kept, together with transfers of names from one to the other. This will lead to endless confusion.

Fifth, the idea of Associate Membership and the paragraph referring thereto are ambiguous. The age when a child should join the church as an active member; whether adults may or may not join as Associate Members; the rights and privileges granted such members; whether persons may have a transfer to another church; all these are left to the discretion of each monthly meeting, and will result in such a variety of action as will weaken the church.

The matter was considered by the Five Years Meeting, but Associate Membership was retained.

In Western Yearly Meeting, of which Plainfield Quarterly Meeting is a part, the matter received careful consideration. The Permanent Board of the Yearly Meeting made the following report:[13]

First, after careful consideration of the subject referred to us, we desire to report that it is our conviction that Western Yearly Meeting has the right to eliminate from its own discipline all sections referring to Associate Membership and to substitute therefor the section from former disciplines establishing Birthright Membership.

Second, if the Yearly Meeting does not so decide, it is our own judgment that the Yearly Meeting should petition the Five Years Meeting, in proper form, for such change as indicated in the request from Plainfield Quarterly Meeting.

Western Yearly Meeting discussed the matter but decided that it would be better not to make such a request to the Five Years Meeting. In the vote taken to return to Birthright Membership, there were seventy-six votes against the motion, and thirty-six for it.

---

12. Minutes of the Five Years Meeting of the American Yearly Meetings of Friends, 1907, pages 18-19.
13. See Minutes of Western Yearly Meeting, 1906.

In an effort to clarify the seeming dissatisfaction with Associate Membership, to explain the reasons for adopting it, and to show its values, the following editorial appeared in *The American Friend*: [14]

The change (from Birthright to Associate Membership) was made because those who drafted the Discipline believed that religion is a personal matter for each soul to settle. The old system seemed to them to encourage formal religion and to treat spiritual life too much as something to be inherited. They did not, however, fly to opposite extremes. They provided for the enrollment of every child in a Friends' family, and they laid upon the church the responsibility for that child's spiritual nurture. But they held that there should come a time in the life of the child when he (or she) should say, by an act of personal choice: "I want to be a Friend"; when, by a positive act of individual faith, he should say: "thy people shall be my people, and thy God shall be my God." The age when this decisive step should be taken is purposely left unsettled in the Discipline. Some children are ready for it at ten or earlier, and others are not ready for it until they have entered upon manhood. It takes often many years of experience—sometimes deep baptisms—to bring them to a full discovery of the power of our faith, and they require much wisdom and patience before their feet are firmly planted on the "highway." Associate Members are put under the especial care and oversight of the pastoral committee of the particular meeting to which they belong. No greater duty, no more sacred business, devolves upon this committee. They, together with the parents, have the responsibility of bringing children from this first stage of membership to the higher stage of personal coöperation in the work and burdens of the church, and it is their duty to decide when the children are ready for active membership.

It is of great interest to note how these statements almost parallel the objections to Birthright Membership. The arguments in favor of Associate Membership seem to eliminate the defects and emphasize the values of Birthright Membership. It is strange, however, that the writer of the above editorial placed the responsibility of membership upon the pastoral committee and parents, and not upon the children themselves.

The great advantages and values of Associate Membership are numerous. They are, of course, dependent upon the individuals who hold such membership.

Associate Membership is practiced in all the Yearly Meetings belonging to the Five Years Meeting. It is also used in Oregon Yearly Meeting. The practice on mission fields is to follow the method of the organizing or supporting yearly meeting.

---

14. Eleventh Month 29, 1906, pages 771-772, "Making Members of the Children."

A COMPARATIVE STUDY OF ASSOCIATE MEMBERSHIP AND BIRTHRIGHT MEMBERSHIPS

THE two methods of membership for children, practiced by the Society of Friends, have many identical elements and some opposing characteristics. These are presented in a parallel study:

Associate Membership	*Birthright Membership*
1. A definite status of membership.	1. The same.
2. Associate Membership may come at birth of child, provided the request is made by the parents, one or both of whom belongs to the Society.	2. Full membership at birth, upon request of parent or parents.
3. Membership is a gift of the Society, until the child reaches the ages of accountability.	3. A gift of the Society for life, unless there is disownment or withdrawal.
4. Requires a personal decision of faith in Christ and belief in the doctrines of Friends, and the public confession of the same.	4. Is continuous and does not require a formal confession of faith, nor is a personal decision required for membership.
5. Conversion or rebirth required.	5. Second Birth emphasized.
6. Associate Membership tends to lead to a vital, religious experience and to active membership.	6. May lead to a cold, nominal membership, or an active one.
7. If at the age of maturity, the person does not show an active interest in the belief and program of the Society, the monthly meeting may remove his name from the list of members.	7. Name may remain on the list of membership, throughout the life of the person, although he may show no interest in the Society.
8. If the person holds the faith of the Society, and wants to apply for active membership he may do so.	8. Birth gives him complete membership.
9. Tends to lead to active membership or complete withdrawal from the church.	9. Leads to active participation, nominal status, or withdrawal from the Society.
10. Makes membership a personal conviction and desire.	10. Makes membership an inheritance.

Associate Membership	*Birthright Membership*
11. Membership is the result of free choice.	11. Membership not the result of free choice, except as the person chooses to stay in the Society.
12. Membership is recruited largely from without the Society.	12. Membership is recruited largely from within the Society.
13. Membership is a goal toward which the person may work.	13. Complete membership is a gift of birth.
14. Associate Membership is a principle or system, and of itself can do nothing. If it is to have real value, it requires great obligations on the part of children, parents and meetings. It requires a continuous, thorough religious education based upon the religion of Jesus, the faith and practice of the Society of Friends, and the abilities and interests of the children.	14. The same.

THE PLACE OF CHILDREN AS ASSOCIATE MEMBERS

UNDER the system of Associate Membership, preparation for active membership becomes an important part in the program of all local meetings. In this respect there is the greatest difference between a meeting which practices Birthright Membership and one which follows Associate Membership.

There are many differences between London, Philadelphia and other meetings which practice Birthright Membership, and those Meetings which belong to the Five Years Meeting and use Associate Membership. In the former, the meetings for worship are based upon silent waiting and freedom. There is no paid minister, "programmed" order of service, nor choir. There may or may not be singing, public praying or speaking. The meeting houses are plain and similar to those of the early days of the Society.

In the Five Years Meeting type there is usually a paid minister, a paid organist and choir director, and frequently a paid director of religious education or an assistant-pastor. In "extreme" meetings a printed bulletin of the service is given out and a vested choir sings a special anthem. There is a definite program and the congregation comes expecting to hear some special music by the choir, and a ser-

133

mon by the minister. Of course, any are free "to take part in the meeting as the Spirit leads." There is a certain freedom which is not found in other denominations. There will be a limited amount of silence, but if there is very much the audience becomes restless and visitors will wonder if something is wrong. At the stated hour the meeting begins, and when the announced program has been completed it is time for the service to close.

Theologically, there is very little difference between the London and the Five Years Meeting types. Both groups reject infant baptism, original sin, predestination; and both emphasize the need of conversion and the second birth. Both believe in peace and social service. The London type places more emphasis on the Inner Light, while the Five Years Meeting type encourages educational evangelism. The former type refers to the Meeting, while the latter commonly uses the terms Friends Church.

In almost every case, the London type of meeting uses Birthright Membership, while the others follow Associate Membership. However, all these differences are not on account of the system of membership of children, but they are the result, almost entirely, of the widespread revivalism which swept the United States during the nineteenth century and which has continued in the twentieth century. The revivals brought many members into the Society of Friends who knew very little about the history and doctrines of Quakerism. They were not accustomed to worshipping in silence and had not been brought into the Society by that method. They required a more active form of service. As the membership grew and conditions changed it was necessary for someone to give full time to the affairs of the meeting. Many of the visiting ministers of the Society were urged to take permanent residence in a local community; a few meetings were bold enough to "hire" a full-time minister, and gradually the pastoral system developed.

The Five Years Meeting discipline provides for certain boards to carry on the work of the united meetings, and some of these were concerned with the work with children. The Board which is particularly interested in the work with children is the Board of Christian Education. Its duties are outlined as follows:[15]

This Board shall be responsible for promoting the work of religious education in the Five Years Meeting, including the editing and supervising of

---

15. Discipline Five Years Meeting of Friends in America (1930), page 87.

our Bible School literature. It shall nominate to the Executive Committee of the Five Years Meeting an editor for our Bible School publications. The Board shall consist of one member from each Yearly Meeting, and five members at large to be appointed by the Five Years Meeting.

Under the system of Associate Membership, two aims direct the activities and thoughts of a local meeting: first, the desire is that all children shall be so interested and instructed that they will be led to the place of personal decision for Christ and the Christian way of life; and secondly, that they will become members of the Society of Friends. The method of achieving these aims is that of educational evangelism.[16] There are two forms of evangelism, revivalism and religious education. Revivalism is practiced in regular sermons by the minister, and in peak times of revivalistic services. Religious education is planned by a local committee on Religious Education, in coöperation with other local committees such as the missionary, peace, prohibition and public morals, music, finance and others. A program is built around the needs, capacities and desires of children and the opportunities and abilities of the meetings. The local monthly meeting uses such agencies as the church school (Sunday or Bible School), the junior church, the junior, and intermediate (or junior high) Christian Endeavor societies, Young Friends groups, missionary societies, Pioneers, Girl Reserves and similar organizations for children. In many meetings there are mid-week programs for the Christian education of children. Children are invited and urged to attend meetings for worship, and frequently they are given opportunity to participate in the worship service. They may attend the business meetings.

One of the outstanding methods of preparing children for active membership is the Pastoral Class. This is a class conducted by the pastor for children of approximately eleven to thirteen years of age, or about the junior high school age level. Such a class is usually held from six to eight weeks before Easter. Special attention is given to a clear presentation of the teachings of Jesus and what it means to be a Christian; and a study of the Friends history, doctrine and organization. At the close of this period, if the children desire and their parents permit, the children are accepted by the monthly meeting as

16. Evangelism is considered as the "Good News of Christ," the Gospel according to Jesus, the acceptance of Jesus as Savior and Guide. There has been a tendency in the Five Years Meeting of Friends to think of evangelism only in the terms of revivalism, to the exclusion of religious education.

members in full, active standing. On Easter Sunday or some other appointed time, the children are "received into full membership" by coming forward and standing before the entire congregation to give witness of their acceptance of the Christian religion, according to the faith of Friends, and "receive the hand of fellowship." From that time on, such children are active members.

⊰VI⊱

CHILDREN AND QUAKERISM

THE SOCIETY OF FRIENDS is a religious fellowship which was developed in England during the seventeenth century. It is an Evangelical group which emphasizes religious freedom, simplicity of worship, and the application of religious ideals to the problems of life. It did not begin as a separate sect, but sought to bring all people to a clear understanding, a complete dedication, and an actual practice of the principles of Jesus. Because the early Friends could not conform to the political, social and religious standards of their day, they suffered serious persecutions and imprisonment. They left a worthy heritage to their successors in consecration to a great ideal, and in an unswerving earnestness in the practical application of that ideal to the problems of life.

Children have always held a high and important place in the theory and practice of the Society of Friends. The family, the meeting and the school have been practical and valuable agencies in the physical, mental, social, moral and spiritual development of children. In the family both the parents and the children had definite responsibilities. The parents held the authority within the home, and the children were expected to obey. All shared in the trials and joys, the obligations and privileges of the family. The basic principle of family life was love, and this directed all the relationships within the home. Servants and apprentices, as well as children, were considered members of the family and they shared in the responsibilities and pleasures of the group.

Children were expected to attend the First-day and week-day meetings for worship. While the services were not planned nor conducted in keeping with the capacities and needs of the children, they attended as a regular part of the affairs of life. Within the family

137

group, religion came first and it always was given preference over anything else. In this way, the children of Friends learned to give a high place to religion. Through association with and imitation of elders who were worthy examples, through the leading of the Inner Light, and by definite instruction, children grew in religious experience.

The Friends, from the earliest days of the Society, held a deep concern for and took special care of the poor, especially the poor children. Likewise, they took particular interest in their apprentices, and developed rules for the system of apprenticeship. Friends were urged to take children into their families as apprentices, and they were expected to give them training in religion, morals, rudiments of learning and a particular trade.

The Friends practiced certain testimonies which they believed led them away from the "vain fashions of the world," into a Christian life according to the Truth. These testimonies included such things as: the simple Quaker garb, the plain language, the use of numerals for the days of the week and the months of the year, the refusal to pay tithes, the refusal to take oaths, hat honor, the belief in peace and in opposition to war, and the practice of silence in worship. The children of Friends shared in these testimonies and were expected to practice them, as far as they were able.

The history of the testimonies of Friends shows that they were prompted by a religious concern. It also reveals the fact that the later Friends disregarded or minimized the importance of many of the testimonies, and in some cases they rejected them entirely. The modern Quaker dresses as other folk do; he has entered into the economic, political and social fields along with his neighbors. Friends, generally, have limited the use of the plain language to the immediate family, Friendly circles, or have done away with it entirely. They no longer stand out as "peculiar" in the matters of dress or speech. Since this is true of the adults, it applies to the children, and their education has been changed in keeping with new ideas. In many communities children attend Friends' schools which emphasize, more or less, the old testimonies, but they do not pride themselves on their differences from the "people of the world."

But where Friends have believed that their testimonies have present religious and social significance, they have maintained them. Illustrative of this point is the continuous emphasis placed upon religious freedom, world peace, and social service. The latter is adequately shown in the child feeding work in Europe and Russia during and since the World War. The children of Friends are taught these humanitarian principles in the home, meeting and school. As they grow into young manhood and womanhood they are given opportunities for the application of these ideals in the throbbing, challenging problems of the social order.

The early Friends developed a theology which has remained fundamentally the same throughout the history of the Society. Children were considered an heritage of the Lord and they were to be brought to a knowledge of and a fellowship with Him.

The theology of the Friends is in great contrast to Calvinism. The latter taught children the theories of total depravity, the sovereignty of God, the utter helplessness of man to aid in his salvation, partial atonement (the theory that Christ died for a select few and not for all), and the supreme and final authority of the Bible as the rule and guide of life. Friends did not approve of these beliefs.

The Friends believed that the child, at birth, was non-moral, and had the capacity for good or evil. Every child had within himself the Inner Light which would lead to the good if its directions were followed. The child was not born a sinner, but he came into the world of sin and became guilty when he himself committed sin. In the natural course of living the child would commit sin and therefore would need to be converted. Conversion was not thought of as a turning away from evil, but rather as an inward, spiritual growth toward the good. It was believed that all children should experience the second birth, and this was a gradual growth which came with following the Inner Light, and the recognition and acceptance of both the inward and outward Christ.

The children of Friends *shared fully,* limited only by their physical, mental, social and religious immaturity, in the religion of their parents. There was but one type of Quakerism and both adults and children were expected to appreciate, accept and apply its principles in their individual lives. The religious experiences of children seem more adult-like than child-like in both phraseology and action. They took such forms as the adoration of God; a mingled emotional response and conflict, sorrow and pleasure; a sense of growth in grace; and a definite otherworldly interest and a belief in immortality. Religion functioned in the practical everyday living of children.

Children, from the beginning of the Society of Friends, have been considered as members. For the first fifty years of the Society membership for both adults and children was of a general and informal nature. To attend the Friends' meetings, to wear the Quaker garb, and to be willing to suffer persecution for Truth's sake were sufficient evidences of membership in the Society. In 1737, London Yearly Meeting adopted a minute which brought a legal membership status, and for children this took the form of Birthright Membership. Children, one or both of whose parents were members, held membership in the Society of Friends from birth. The system of Birthright Membership became a subject of great controversy soon after its adoption, and it is still open to criticism. There have been two definite results from the conflict: the continuation of the system of Birthright Membership as the method of membership for children by some yearly meetings; and the rejection of it by other yearly meetings and the substitution of Associate Membership.

The attitudes toward children, in the meetings using the different types of membership, are quite similar. Meetings using either system are greatly concerned that children shall become active and not nominal members and both seek to make children Friends in fact as well as in name. The meetings which use Birthright Membership are inclined to place great reliance upon the leading of the Inner Light and a gradual growth in religious experience; while meetings which practice Associate Membership are divided into two groups, those which rely upon revivalism, and those which emphasize religious education. However, all three methods, the Inner Light, revivalism, and religious education are commonly practiced by the different groups of Friends.

There are many forward-looking principles in the early Friends philosophy and practice of education. There were two general aims of education: first, to instruct and train boys and girls in the faith and practice of the Society of Friends, so that they might live noble Christian lives and be prepared for a future state of existence; and second, to give worthy instruction and opportunities for personal experience and growth in religion, morals, secular education and manual arts.

The doctine of the Inner Light has great possibilities for creative education. It gives rise to original ideas, and if followed it leads to constructive, individual achievement.

The Friends were leaders in two fields of education, namely, education of the poor and education in manual arts. They believed that the advantages of education should be given to all children, and if parents were too poor to send their children to school, the meeting to which they belonged should make it possible for them to attend. Consequently, in the early days of the Society of Friends, most of the local meetings conducted schools, and rich and poor alike received an education. The Friends held that all children regardless of financial or social position should be taught some useful employment. This type of education was a forerunner of our modern vocational education. The Friends believed in the theory of "learning by doing" and they gave practical and continuous opportunities for education in the manual arts in the home and school.

The greatest religious educational contribution of the Friends was the belief that religion was an integral part and a motivating force in all education. Teachers who were members of the Society were selected to instruct the children. The reading of the Bible, silent or vocal prayer, and definite instruction in religion according to the Truth as held by the Friends, were parts of the regular system of education. In the early seventeenth century the Friends emphasized the place of religion in educational theory and practice in a similar way to the modern approach to the subject.

Friends had a keen insight into the value of religion and a far-sighted vision as to its place in education when they insisted that it was an integrating force in life. They made no apologies, nor did they need to do so, for the belief that religion was an active, dynamic element in life. They believed that the ideals of Jesus should be the guiding forces in all activities—religious, educational, social, moral, commercial and political. Their first allegiance was to God and they believed that through the leading of the Inner Light, He would guide them into the good life. It should be remembered that Friends did not belittle moral or secular education, but it is true that they emphasized the belief that the fundamental and basic principle in all education was religion.

Another important factor in Friends education was the great emphasis placed upon the home, the meeting and the school as educational agencies. This was a part of their synoptic view of life, and the belief that education was a continuous, coöperative process.

There were, also, certain backward tendencies in the Friends philosophy of education. In keeping with the views of their day, the early Friends had no clearly defined child psychology. Education was not child-centered. The chief purpose of education was to train children so that they would be good members of the Society of Friends. Children were expected to share as fully as possible in the theories and practice of the adults. There was very little place for informal, creative education. The principles of directed freedom and life-centered situations were practically unknown.

One of the greatest weaknesses of early Quaker education was the principle of guarded education. This theory was inconsistent with the doctrine of the Inner Light; it was too limited in both material and method; it emphasized indoctrination; and it eliminated the principles of freedom and creativity. In theory the desire to train children in accordance with a definite philosophy or theology has certain values, but if it leads to a complete indoctrination without the freedom of evaluation and the power of choice, it is poor educational procedure. Among the Friends it tended to lead toward a narrow sectarianism which undoubtedly led to the quietism and complacency of the Society in the eighteenth century. The Friends had the right to hold convictions and they should have had the privilege to present those convictions to their children, but most of the values were limited unless the children, upon reaching the age of accountability, had the opportunity to choose for themselves.

If the theory and methods of the early Quaker religious education for children had continued to develop, the story of religious education and the Society of Friends itself might have been different. They had the seed which might have blossomed forth into the fruits of modern religious education. It is at least fair to say that the early Friends hold an important place in the theory back of our present religious educational philosophy, and that the history of religious education must give place to their educational philosophy and activities.

The place of children in the theory and practice of the Society of Friends at the present time is, in many respects, similar to the position given them in the seventeenth century. The Friends have eliminated many undesirable elements such as adult standards for children, and a narrow guarded education; and they have retained the great values in doctrine, educational theories and social participation. They have taken into account the modern psychological and educational principles. The Friends meeting of the London type may have a modern system of religious education. The First-day school may follow all the advantages of modern religious education with a graded program of worship, instruction and service. The publishing agencies of both of the Philadelphia Yearly Meetings have developed some excellent courses of study graded according to modern educational and psychological principles, and they present the Friends' doctrines for the children. In this way, the First-day school helps meet the religious needs of children. In London and the Philadelphia Yearly Meetings there are elementary schools for the education of children, and in these schools religious education is given an important place.

In the earlier days of the Society of Friends, those meetings which later formed the Five Years Meeting conducted elementary and secondary schools as well as colleges. With the development of the public school system of the United States, these Friends closed their elementary and most of the secondary schools and sent their children to the public schools. This fact increases the obligation of religious education for the Five Years Meeting of Friends.

The Five Years Meeting Friends accepted the evangelistic and revivalistic methods of the nineteenth and twentieth centuries, and the religious educational movement of the twentieth century. At the present time most of the meetings use the graded and correlated program of religious education. In this way the capacities, interests and needs of children are given careful consideration and ample opportunity for development. Many Friends' Yearly Meetings are active in the International Council of Religious Education, and follow its program through the Board of Religious Education of the Five Years Meeting and local meeting and yearly meeting boards or committees of religious education. They are also affiliated with local and state councils of religious education. They coöperate with other denominations and movements in the broader program of religious education and in these ways the children of Friends are given the best opportunities for religious growth.

In all the philosophy and activity of the Society of Friends, children hold a place of supreme importance. In the membership, theology, education and institutions, children are fully incorporated into the life of the Society. This is the place of children in the theory and practice of the Society of Friends—called Quakers.

BIBLIOGRAPHY

BOOKS

Alexander, Helen Cadbury. *Richard Cadbury of Birmingham*, London, 1906.

Barclay, John. *Some Account of the Life of Joseph Pike, of Cork in Ireland, Who died in the year 1729. Written by Himself.* Edited by John Barclay, London, 1837.

Barclay, Robert. *A Catechism and Confession of Faith*, (1673),[1] Philadelphia, 1843.
An Apology for the True Christian Divinity, being an Explanation and Vindication of the Principles and Doctrines of the People called Quakers, (1675), Philadelphia, 1850.

Barclay, Robert (of Reigate). *On Membership in the Society of Friends*, London, 1872.
The Inner Life of the Religious Societies of the Commonwealth: considered principally with Reference to the Influence of Church Organization on the Spread of Christianity, London, 1877.

Bellers, John. *Proposals for Raising a College of Industry of all Useful Trades and Husbandry with Profit for the Rich, a Plentiful Living for the Poor, and a Good Education for Youth, which will be Advantage to the Government, by the Increase of the People and their Riches*, London, 1695.

Benezet, Anthony. *A Pattern of Christian Education*, Germantown, 1756.

Best, Mary Agnes. *Rebel Saints*, New York, 1925.

Bevans, John. *A Brief View of the Doctrines of the Christian Religion as professed by the Society of Friends, in the Form of Questions and Answers, for the Instruction of Youth*, Philadelphia, 1843.

Bickley, A. C. *George Fox and the Early Quakers*, London, 1884.

Braithwaite, Joseph B. *Memoirs of Joseph J. Gurney; with selections from His Journal and Correspondence*, Volumes I and II, Edited by Joseph B. Braithwaite, Philadelphia, 1854.

Braithwaite, William C. *The Beginnings of Quakerism*, London, 1912.
The Second Period of Quakerism, London, 1919.

---

1. Numbers in parentheses indicate the date of the first editions.

Brayshaw, A. Neave. *The Quakers, Their Story and Message,* London, 1927.

Broomell, Anna Pettit. *The Children's Story Garden, Collected by a Committee of Philadelphia Yearly Meeting of Friends,* Philadelphia, 1920.

Budd, Thomas. *Good Order Established in Pennsylvania and New Jersey in America,* Philadelphia, 1685.

Budge, Frances A. *The Barclays of Ury and Other Sketches of the Early Friends,* London, 1881.

Burrough, Edward. *The Memorable Works of a Son of Thunder and Consolation: namely that True Prophet and Faithful Servant of God, and Sufferer for the Testimony of Jesus,* London, 1672.

Clarkson, Thomas. *A Portraiture of Quakerism, as taken from a View of the Moral Education, Discipline, Peculiar Customs, Religious Principles, Political and Civil Economy, and Character of the Society of Friends,* Volumes I, II, and III, London, 1806.

Dillingham, John H. *What shall I do with my Inherited Membership?* Philadelphia, 1889.

Dorland, Arthur G. *A History of the Society of Friends (Quakers) in Canada,* Toronto, 1927.

Dudley, Robert. *In My Youth,* Indianapolis, 1914.

Elkinton, Joseph S. *Selections from the Diary and Correspondence of Joseph S. Elkinton,* Philadelphia, 1913.

Emmott, Elizabeth B. *A Short History of Quakerism (Earlier Periods),* London, 1923.

Evans, Thomas. *A Concise Account of the Religious Society of Friends, Commonly called Quakers; Embracing a Sketch of Their Christian Doctrines and Practices,* Philadelphia, no date.

Evans, William and Thomas. *Edward Burrough, a Memoir of a Faithful Servant of Christ and Minister of the Gospel, Who died at Newgate, 14th, 12 month, 1662,* London, 1851.

Evans, Thomas, *Examples of Youthful Piety; Principally intended for the Instruction of Young Persons,* Philadelphia, 1851.

Forster, Joseph. *Piety Promoted in Brief Biographical Memorials of some of the Religious Society of Friends, Commonly called Quakers.* The Eleventh Part, Philadelphia, 1830.

Fox, George. *An Autobiography.* Edited by Rufus M. Jones, Philadelphia, 1919.
A Catechism for Children, London, 1657.
A Warning to all Teachers of Children which are called School-masters and Mistresses and to Parents, London, 1657.
To all School-masters, Priests and Teachers and Magistrates that be Christians, London, 1660.

The Works of George Fox, in Eight Volumes, Philadelphia, 1831.
—Volumes I and II. *A Journal or Historical Account of the Life, Travels, Sufferings, Christian Experiences and Labour of Love in the Work of the Ministry, of that Ancient, Eminent, and Faithful Servant of Jesus Christ, George Fox.*
—Volume III. *The Great Mystery of the Great Whore Unfolded; and Anti-Christ's Kingdom Revealed unto Destruction.*
—Volumes IV, V, and VI. *Gospel Truth Demonstrated, in a Collection of Doctrinal Books, given forth by that Faithful Minister of Jesus Christ, George Fox: containing Principles Essential to Christianity and Salvation Held Among the People called Quakers.*
—Volumes VII and VIII. *A Collection of Many Select and Christian Epistles, Letters and Testimonies, written on Sundry Occasions, by that Ancient, Eminent, Faithful Friend and Minister of Christ Jesus, George Fox.*

Fox, George, and Ellis Hookes. *Instruction for Right Spelling, Reading and Writing*, London, 1697.

Fox, George, John Stubs, Benjamin Furley. *The Battle-Door for Teachers and Professors to Learn Singular and Plural*, London, 1660.

Freame, John. *Scripture Instruction in the Form of Question and Answer as taught in the Royal Lancasterian Schools; being a Selection Designed to Promote Piety and Virtue; and discourage Vice and Immorality*, (1713), London, 1813.

Freame, John, and Anthony Purver. *Counsel to Friends' Children on Education*, London, 1799.

Friends Library, The. Comprising Journals, Doctrinal Treatises, and Other Writings of Members of the Society of Friends. Edited by William and Thomas Evans, Fourteen Volumes, Philadelphia, 1837.

Gough, John. *A History of the People called Quakers, from Their first Rise to the present Time. Compiled from Authentic Records and from the Writings of that People*, Volumes I, II, III and IV, Dublin, 1789.

Graham, John W. *The Divinity of Man*, London, 1927.
The Faith of a Quaker, Cambridge, 1920.

Gummere, Amelia M. *The Journal of John Woolman*, New York, 1922.

Gurney, Joseph John. *Thoughts on Habit and Discipline*, London, 1852.

Harris, Helen B. *The Basis of Membership in the Society of Friends*, London, no date.

Harris, J. Rendel. *New Appreciations of George Fox. A Tercentenary Collection of Studies*, London, 1925.

Hicks, Elias. *Journal of the Life and Religious Labours of Elias Hicks*, New York, 1832.

Hodgkin, Lucy Violet. *A Book of Quaker Saints*, London, 1918.

Janney, Samuel M. *Conversations on Religious Subjects between a Father and His Two Sons,* Philadelphia, 1835.
Memoirs of Samuel M. Janney, a Minister of the Religious Society of Friends, Philadelphia, 1881.
The Life of George Fox; with Dissertations on His Views concerning the Doctrines, Testimonies, and Discipline of the Christian Church, Philadelphia, 1853.

Jay, Allen. *Autobiography of Allen Jay,* Philadelphia, 1910.

Jones, Lester. *Quakerism in Action. Recent Humanitarian and Reform Activities of the American Quakers, with an Introduction by Rufus M. Jones,* New York, 1929.

Jones, Louis T. *The Quakers of Iowa,* Iowa City, 1914.

Jones, Rufus M. *The Faith and Practice of the Quakers,* London, 1927.
Finding the Trail of Life, New York, 1931.
The Inner Life, New York, 1916.
The Later Periods of Quakerism, Volumes I and II, London, 1921.
(Assisted by Isaac Sharpless and Amelia M. Gummere). *The Quakers in the American Colonies,* London, 1911.
Religious Foundations, New York, 1923.
Spiritual Energies in Daily Life, New York, 1922.
Spiritual Reformers in the 16th and 17th Centuries, London, 1914.
The World Within, New York, 1918.

Kendall, John. *Letters on Religious Subjects written by Divers Friends,* Philadelphia, 1831.

Klain, Zora. *Quaker Contributions to Education in North Carolina,* Philadelphia, 1924.

Moon, James H. *Why Friends (Quakers) do not Baptize with Water,* Fallsington, Pennsylvania, 1909.

Moon, John. *Observations and Quotations on Obtaining Church Membership by a Natural Birth and Education,* Stokesley, 1815.

Nayler, James. *A Collection of Sundry Books, Epistles, and Papers written by James Nayler some of which were never before printed, with an Impartial Revelation of the most Remarkable Transactions Relating to His Life,* London, 1716.

Parrish, Edward. *Education in the Society of Friends, Past, Present and Prospective,* Philadelphia, 1865.

Penington, Isaac. *Letters of Isaac Penington Son of Alderman Penington of London, and an Eminent Minister of the Gospel in the Society of Friends, which He joined in the Year 1658,* Philadelphia, 1842.
The Works of Isaac Penington, a Minister of the Gospel in the Society of Friends, Volumes I, II, III and IV, (1681), Philadelphia, 1863.

Penn, William. *A Brief Account of the Rise and Progress of the People called Quakers, in which Their Fundamental Principles, Doctrines, Worship, Ministry and Discipline are plainly declared,* (1694), Philadelphia, 1849.

A Collection of the Works of William Penn, in two volumes, to which is prefixed a Journal of His Life, with many Original Letters and Papers not before published, London, 1726.

Charters of the Public School Founded by Charter in the Town and County of Philadelphia, 1701, 1708 and 1711, Philadelphia, no date.

Extracts from the Advice to His Children, London, 1819.

No Cross, No Crown. A Discourse showing the Nature and Discipline of the Holy Cross of Christ: and that the Denial of Self, and Daily Bearing of Christ's Cross is the Alone Way of the Rest and Kingdom of God, to which are added the Living and Dying Testimonies of Many Persons of Fame and Learning, both of Ancient and Modern Times in Favour of this Treatise, (1668), Philadelphia, 1845.

Penney, Norman. *The Journal of George Fox.* Tercentenary Edition, London, 1924.

The First Publishers of Truth. Early Records collected in 1720, London, 1907.

Phipps, Joseph. *A Dissertation on the Nature and Effect of Christian Baptism,* New York, 1837.

The Original and Present State of Man, Briefly considered, wherein is shown the Nature of His Fall, and the Necessity, Means, and Manner of his Restoration through the Sacrifice of Christ, and the sensible Operation of that Divine Principle of Grace and Truth, Held forth to the World by the People called Quakers, to which is added some Remarks on the Doctrine of Predestination, the Scriptures, Worship and the Kingdom of Heaven, (1767), Philadelphia, 1876.

Rowntree, John S. *Quakerism, Past and Present: being an Inquiry into the Causes of its Decline in Great Britain and Ireland,* London, 1859.

Sewell, William. *The History of the Rise, Increase and Progress of the Christian People Called Quakers, Intermixed with several Remarkable Occurrences* (first English edition, 1725), Volumes I and II, in one volume, New York, 1844.

Sharpless, Isaac. *The Quaker Boy on the Farm and at School,* Philadelphia, 1908.

Smith, Joseph. *A Descriptive Catalog of Friends Books, or Books written by the Members of the Society of Friends, from Their first Rise to the present Time,* Volumes I and II, and Supplement, London, 1867.

Stephen, Caroline E. *Quaker Strongholds,* London, 1891.

Story, Thomas. *A Journal of the Life of Thomas Story, containing an Account of his Remarkable Convincement of, and Embracing the Principles of Truth as Held by the People called Quakers; and also His Travels and Labours in the Service of the Gospel,* New Castle Upon Tyne, 1747.

Thomas, Allen C. and Richard H. *A History of the Friends in America.* Philadelphia, 1905.

Thomas, Edward. *Quaker Adventures: Experiences of Twenty-three Adventurers in International Understanding,* New York, 1928.

Tuke, Henry. *The Principles of Religion as Professed by the Society of Christians usually called Quakers. Written for the Instruction of Their Youth and for the Information of Strangers,* London, 1805.

Tuke, Samuel. *Memoirs of the Life of Stephen Crisp with Selections from His Works,* York, 1824.
Memoirs of George Whitehead; a Minister of the Gospel in the Society of Friends: Being the Substance of the Account of His Life, written by Himself, and published after his Decease in the year 1725, under the Title of "His Christian Progress," with an Appendix containing a Selection from His Other Works, Volumes I and II, Philadelphia, 1832.

Tyler, B. B. *American Church History Series, Volume XII, "The Society of Friends"* by A. C. Thomas, New York, 1894.

Willmott, H. C. (Inheritor). *The Quaker Inheritance: What Should be done with It?* London, 1903.

Woody, Thomas. *Early Quaker Education in Pennsylvania,* New York, 1920.
Quaker Education in the Colony and State of New Jersey; a Source Book, Philadelphia, 1923.
A Journal of the Life, Gospel Labours, and Christian Experiences of that Faithful Minister of Jesus Christ, John Woolman, to which are added His Last Epistle and Other Writings, (1774), Philadelphia, 1845.
Serious Considerations on Various Subjects of Importance, (1773), New York, 1805.

Woolman, John. *A First Book for Children,* Wilmington, 1774.

Wright, Luella M. *Literature and Education in Early Quakerism,* Iowa City, 1933.
The Literary Life of the Early Friends, 1650 to 1725, New York, 1932.

A Collection of Christian and Brotherly Advices given forth from Time to Time by the Yearly Meeting of Friends for Pennsylvania and New Jersey, Handwritten, 1763.

Advices and Rules agreed to by the Yearly Meeting of Friends in Ireland, Dublin, 1811.

Advices and Discipline. Supplement to the Rules of Discipline of the Religious Society of Friends with Advices, London, 1849.

Book of Discipline agreed on by the Yearly Meeting of Friends for New England, Providence, 1785.

Book of Christian Discipline of the Religious Society of Friends in Great Britain, London, 1883.

Book of Discipline of New York Yearly Meeting of the Religious Society of Friends, General Conference Affiliation (Hicksite), Revised 1930, New York, 1930.

Christian Advices of Philadelphia Yearly Meeting, Philadelphia, 1808.

Christian and Brotherly Advices given forth from Time to Time by the Yearly Meeting in London, from 1672 to 1761, Handwritten, 1761.

Christian and Brotherly Advices given forth by the Yearly Meeting in London, from 1688 to 1769, Handwritten, 1769.

Christian Advices issued by the Yearly Meeting of Friends held in Philadelphia, Philadelphia, 1879.

Christian Discipline of London Yearly Meeting of the Religious Society of Friends, consisting of Extracts on Doctrine, Practice, and Church Government from the Epistles and other Documents issued under the Sanction of London Yearly Meeting, 1672 to 1917, Three Parts: I. Christian Doctrine, 1883; II. Christian Practice, 1911; III. Church Government, 1917, London, 1917.

Constitution and Discipline for the American Yearly Meetings. Adopted by New York Yearly Meeting of the Religious Society of Friends in 1901, New York, 1901.

Discipline of the Society of Friends of New York Yearly Meeting. Revised and Adopted by the Meeting held in New York in 1859, New York, 1859.

Discipline of the Yearly Meeting of the Religious Society of Friends held in New York; for the State of New York and Parts Adjacent. Revised in 1872, New York, 1872.

Discipline of the Yearly Meeting of the Religious Society of Friends, New York, Revised, 1872, New York, 1878.

Discipline, Being the Constitution and Discipline of the Five Years Meeting of the Friends in America, Richmond, 1924.

Discipline, Being the Constitution and Discipline of the Five Years Meeting of Friends in America, Richmond, 1930.

Epistles from the Yearly Meeting of Friends, held in London, to the Quarterly and Monthly Meetings in Great Britain, Ireland, and Elsewhere, from 1681 to 1817 inclusive: with an introduction comprising an Account of Several Preceding Epistles and of the Early Records of the Yearly Meeting; also an Index to some of the Principal Matters, London, 1818.

Epistles from the Yearly Meeting of Friends held in London to the Quarterly and Monthly Meetings in Great Britain, Ireland, and Elsewhere, from 1681 to 1857 inclusive: with an Historical Introduction and a Chapter comprising some of the Early Epistles and Records of the Yearly Meeting, Volumes I and II, London, 1858.

Extracts from the Minutes and Advices of the Yearly Meeting of Friends held in London from its first Institution, (the first printed discipline), London, 1783.

Faith and Practice of the Religious Society of Friends of Philadelphia and Vicinity. A Book of Christian Discipline approved by the Yearly Meeting held at Fourth and Arch Streets, Philadelphia, 1926.

Rules of Discipline of Philadelphia Yearly Meeting, Handwritten, 1704.

Rules of Discipline and Christian Advices of the Yearly Meeting of Friends for Pennsylvania and New Jersey, Philadelphia, 1797.

Rules of Discipline of the Religious Society of Friends, with Advices, London, 1834.

Rules of Discipline of the Yearly Meeting of Friends for Pennsylvania, New Jersey, Delaware and the Eastern Parts of Maryland. Revised and Adopted by the Said Meeting, held in Philadelphia by adjournment from the 21st of the Fourth month to the 26th of the same inclusive, 1834, Philadelphia, 1873.

Griffith, John. *Some Brief Remarks upon Sundry Important Subjects necessary to be Understood and Attended to by all Professing the Christian Religion. Principally addressed to the People called Quakers*, London, 1764.

Grubb, Edward. *The Evangelical Movement and its Impact on the Society of Friends*, Leominster, 1924.

Hall, David. *An Epistle of Love and Caution to the Quarterly and Monthly Meetings of Friends in Great Britain and Elsewhere*, London, 1748.

Holme, Benjamin. *An Epistle of Tender Counsel to Parents, School-masters and School-mistresses; and likewise to the Youth*, London, 1749.

Philadelphia Yearly Meeting. *The Ancient Testimony of the Religious Society of Friends commonly called Quakers, Respecting some of Their Christian Doctrines and Practices. Revised and given forth by the Yearly Meeting held in Philadelphia in the Fourth Month*, (1843), Philadelphia, 1843.

Robinson, A. *An Epistle of Tender Caution and Advice to Friends, especially the Youth*, London, 1751.

Rutty, John. *The Liberty of the Spirit and of the Flesh Distinguished; in an Address to those Captive in Spirit among the People called Quakers, who are commonly called Libertines*, Dublin, 1759.

Tract Association of Friends. *A Series of Tracts on Moral and Religious Subjects*, Volumes I, II, and III, Philadelphia, 1876. Tract number:

1. Memoirs of John Woolman.
6. Christian Instruction; in a Dialogue as between a Mother and her Daughter.
11. Religious Duties.
17. Hints to Parents on the Subject of Education.
21. Address to Those who have the Care of children.
27. On the Holy Scriptures.
44. Memoir of Sarah Lidbetter, aged Nine and a half.
60. On Baptism.
65. Salvation by Jesus Christ.
66. On Theatrical Amusements.
98. Robert Barclay.
105. Little Children: A Short Account of Benny White and Hannah Dingle.
109. The Kingdom of God Within.

118. On Prayer.

120. On the Love of God.

121. On the Fear of God.

123. On Public Worship.

125. On Watchfulness and Waiting upon God.

Tract Association of Friends. *Biographical Sketches and Anecdotes of Members of the Religious Society of Friends,* Philadelphia, 1870.
Memoirs and Essays on Moral and Religious Subjects, Volumes I and II, Philadelphia, no date.
The Moral Almanac of 1852, Philadelphia, 1852.
Musings and Memories, Being Chiefly a Collection of Anecdotes and Reflections of a Religious Character on Various Subjects, Philadelphia, 1875.

The American Friend
(Published at Philadelphia and Richmond)

The British Friend
(London)

AUTHOR, TITLE OF ARTICLE	VOLUME	YEAR	PAGE
Forbush, Bliss. *The Aims of Religious Education and our First Day School Program.*	85	1928	347
Burke, Frances H. *Children and Mystical Religion.*	88	[142, 165, 187, 1931 205, 225	
Rawson, Edward B. *On Birthright Membership.*	89	1932	509

The Friends Quarterly Examiner
(London)

Balkwill, Helen. *Birthright Membership.*[2]		1871	524
Fowler, A. F. *Church Membership.*		1875	355
Sturge, Matilda. *On Conversion in Relation to Membership.*		1876	104
Fowler, Ann F. *Some Remarks Bearing on Birthright Membership.*		1887	25
Brown, Alfred W. *Our Younger Members.*	25	1891	43
Bennett, Alfred W. *et al. A Symposium on Birthright Membership.*	30	1896	239-269
Pumphrey, Mary. *Birthright Membership.*	54	1920	225
Rowntree, Joseph S. *et al. The Basis of Membership of the Society of Friends*	55	1921	18-55

The Friends Review
(Philadelphia)

Fox, J. J. *Birthright Membership.*	14	1861	468
W. E. H. *Thoughts on Birthright Membership.*	20	1867	198
Balkwill, Helen. *Birthright Membership.*	25	1871	260
Wing, Edward. *Birthright Membership.*	32	1878	290

The Journal of the Friends Historical Society
(London)

Axon, William E. A. *Some Quaker Teachers in 1736.*	5	1908	47
Miller, William F. *Early Friends Schools in Scotland.*	7	1910	105
No author given. *A School in Ilchester Jail*, 1662.			16
Fox, Margaret. *Margaret Fox to Her Grandchildren* .	12	1915	146

2. Volume numbers were not given until 1889.

INDEX

161

Family in America

AN ARNO PRESS / NEW YORK TIMES COLLECTION

Abbott, John S. C. **The Mother at Home:** Or, The Principles of Maternal Duty. 1834.

Abrams, Ray H., editor. **The American Family in World War II.** 1943.

Addams, Jane. **A New Conscience and an Ancient Evil.** 1912.

The Aged and the Depression: Two Reports, 1931–1937. 1972.

Alcott, William A. **The Young Husband.** 1839.

Alcott, William A. **The Young Wife.** 1837.

American Sociological Society. **The Family.** 1909.

Anderson, John E. **The Young Child in the Home.** 1936.

Baldwin, Bird T., Eva Abigail Fillmore and Lora Hadley. **Farm Children.** 1930.

Beebe, Gilbert Wheeler. **Contraception and Fertility in the Southern Appalachians.** 1942.

Birth Control and Morality in Nineteenth Century America: Two Discussions, 1859–1878. 1972.

Brandt, Lilian. **Five Hundred and Seventy-Four Deserters and Their Families.** 1905. Baldwin, William H. **Family Desertion and Non-Support Laws.** 1904.

Breckinridge, Sophonisba P. **The Family and the State:** Select Documents. 1934.

Calverton, V. F. **The Bankruptcy of Marriage.** 1928.

Carlier, Auguste. **Marriage in the United States.** 1867.

Child, [Lydia]. **The Mother's Book.** 1831.

Child Care in Rural America: Collected Pamphlets, 1917–1921. 1972.

Child Rearing Literature of Twentieth Century America, 1914–1963. 1972.

The Colonial American Family: Collected Essays, 1788–1803. 1972.

Commander, Lydia Kingsmill. The American Idea. 1907.

Davis, Katharine Bement. Factors in the Sex Life of Twenty-Two Hundred Women. 1929.

Dennis, Wayne. The Hopi Child. 1940.

Epstein, Abraham. Facing Old Age. 1922. New Introduction by Wilbur J. Cohen.

The Family and Social Service in the 1920s: Two Documents, 1921–1928. 1972.

Hagood, Margaret Jarman. Mothers of the South. 1939.

Hall, G. Stanley. Senescence: The Last Half of Life. 1922.

Hall, G. Stanley. Youth: Its Education, Regimen, and Hygiene. 1904.

Hathway, Marion. The Migratory Worker and Family Life. 1934.

Homan, Walter Joseph. Children & Quakerism. 1939.

Key, Ellen. The Century of the Child. 1909.

Kirchwey, Freda. Our Changing Morality: A Symposium. 1930.

Kopp, Marie E. Birth Control in Practice. 1934.

Lawton, George. New Goals for Old Age. 1943.

Lichtenberger, J. P. Divorce: A Social Interpretation. 1931.

Lindsey, Ben B. and Wainwright Evans. The Companionate Marriage. 1927. New Introduction by Charles Larsen.

Lou, Herbert H. Juvenile Courts in the United States. 1927.

Monroe, Day. Chicago Families. 1932.

Mowrer, Ernest R. Family Disorganization. 1927.

Reed, Ruth. The Illegitimate Family in New York City. 1934.

Robinson, Caroline Hadley. Seventy Birth Control Clinics. 1930.

Watson, John B. Psychological Care of Infant and Child. 1928.

White House Conference on Child Health and Protection. The Home and the Child. 1931.

White House Conference on Child Health and Protection. The Adolescent in the Family. 1934.

Young, Donald, editor. The Modern American Family. 1932.